Foul Deeds and Suspicious De

NEWCASTLE

MAUREEN ANDERSON

Series Editor
Brian Elliott

Wharncliffe Books

First Published in 2004 by
Wharncliffe Books
an imprint of
Pen and Sword Books Limited,
47 Church Street, Barnsley,
South Yorkshire. S70 2AS

Copyright © Maureen Anderson, 2004

For up-to-date information on other titles produced under the
Wharncliffe imprint, please telephone or write to:

Wharncliffe Books
FREEPOST
47 Church Street
Barnsley
South Yorkshire S70 2BR
Telephone (24 hours): 01226 - 734555

ISBN: 1-903425-34-4

A CIP catalogue record of this book is available from the
British Library

Cover design: Jonathan Wilkinson

Printed in the United Kingdom by
CPI UK

Contents

Introduction

Rivers were a source of water, food and a transportation route for trade. Wherever there was a large river, from Roman times and earlier, people made temporary and then more permanent homes on its banks. The River Tyne was what gave Newcastle its beginnings and later its prosperity. In the first history published on the town in 1649 by Camden, Newcastle is described as *Ocellus*, the Eye of the North. Daniel Defoe referred to the town in 1775 as a 'spacious, extended, infinitely populous place.' In 1778 C T Middleton, in his geography of the town, described it as 'ancient, large, disagreeable and dirty, but extremely populous and very rich' and in 1875 Samuel Smiles wrote that 'Newcastle has been converted into a busy centre of commerce.' All these descriptions were true. Certainly by the early eighteenth century the town was the most important in the North East. Newcastle, from its beginnings, developed industry very quickly and it also became a prosperous commercial centre. Coal deposits nearby made it possible to manufacture glass. Glass, coal, soap and salt were transported from the town in sailing vessels via the river and then the sea. From the birth of the town Newcastle had its share of very wealthy merchants and later, ironworks, shipbuilding and other industries too numerous to mention, brought wealth to many more. This industry brought a pall of dense fog that always seemed to hover over the rooftops of the town giving even the most beautiful buildings a grey, dirty appearance. Around Newcastle there were the natural resources of coal, lead and iron which meant that the resulting mines were a huge boost to the economy. Although there was great wealth both in and around Newcastle, there was also the other side of the coin, the workforce that laboured within these industries and lived in the local villages and towns.

A report on the sanitary conditions in Newcastle compiled in 1839 by John Walsham stated:

There are a considerable number of lodging-houses in Newcastle, some of the rooms of which are frequently occupied by from 15 to 20 persons each. In these houses the most deplorable scenes of profligacy and depravity are met, with both sexes being crowded together in a manner injurious to both health and morals.

Shirley Brooks wrote in the *Morning Chronicle* in October 1849:

The houses of the pit village may be divided into three classes. Those of the lowest class usually contain only one room; those of the second contain a large room and attic. The best houses consist of two rooms on the ground floor, with generally an attic over one of them. In all cases, the sitting room door is the street door.

More than one half the pit populations virtually live-each family-in a single room. Here is bedroom and kitchen-here the men and boys, on their return from the pit, wash their almost naked bodies, too often in the presence of growing-up daughters and sisters and here too the women wash and undress.

Most of the working classes could not read or write so illiteracy, poverty and the living conditions combined as a perfect recipe for crime.

There were plenty of public houses where cheap drink could be consumed and, for a while, one could relax and forget about the daily drudge. Over indulgence in alcohol brought problems. Brawls, theft, domestic violence and murder were an all too common by-product of a good session in the local beerhouse or inn. It was not just the men who would sit in a beerhouse all day and spend their wages; many of the women did the same. The children would be left to their own devices and some would go hungry because there was no money left for food.

Punishment for any kind of crime was usually swift if not always just. The castle once held felons chained to the walls of the dungeon. Newgate was the common gaol from 1400 to 1823 when it was demolished and a new prison built. The conditions within the prison were appalling. Felons were also often tried and imprisoned at Morpeth. Public executions in

Newcastle usually took place either on the Town Moor or Westgate, and in Morpeth either in the gaol or on Fair Moor. The hangings would be watched by hundreds of spectators and the body was often given to the surgeons for dissection. Dissection of a criminal's body was abolished in 1832 and public hangings ceased in 1868.

Transportation for a number of years, if not for life, was another common punishment. The severest sentence could be carried out for burglary, coining (forgery), sheep stealing and highway robbery as well as the more serious crimes of rape and murder. These sentences, however, did not seem to act as any sort of a deterrent because, as in other densely populated industrial towns, crime was rife. It should be noted that in many cases the sentence imposed was given, not for the severity of the crime, but seemed to depend on who the victim was and how he or she conducted themselves. The murder of one's wife or of a prostitute was not usually considered as serious as robbing a gentleman. Men controlled the justice system, as women, especially of the working and lower classes, were considered inferior and not capable of making important decisions.

Painstaking research of historical documents, court records, books and newspapers has produced a book of events, many of them little publicized or long forgotten, that span four centuries. Although some of these tales may make your blood run cold, spare a thought, not only for the victims, but the circumstances that surrounded the lives of these people that were a factor in causing these terrible deeds to be carried out.

Foul Deeds and Suspicious Deaths In & Around Newcastle is part of a popular, ever-growing series that is published by Wharncliffe Books and I have thoroughly enjoyed being part of the team in its production. I would like to acknowledge, with gratitude, the people that have given their help and support including Brian Elliott, Series Editor and the team at Wharncliffe, the staff of Hartlepool Reference Library whose assistance I have found invaluable, the staff of the Local Studies Department at Newcastle Library and also Jim, my husband and friend, for his patience.

CHAPTER 1

The Witch Hunt
1649

A mention of a petition in the common council books of Newcastle dated 26 March 1649 concerning witches was signed by many of the inhabitants of the town. The consequence of this petition was that all suspected witches were arrested and brought to trial.

Magistrates of Newcastle sent two of their sergeants, Thomas Shevill and Cuthbert Nicholson, to Scotland to ask a supposed witch-finder to come to Newcastle to officiate in deciding whether the accused were indeed witches. The Scotsman, who was not named in the records, was offered his travel costs to and from Scotland and the sum of 20s (£1) for each witch that was condemned. The so-called reputable

A woman is being searched for the 'Devil's mark' by being pricked with pins to determine whether or not she is a witch. Author's collection

witch-finder claimed that his tried and true method of pinpricking was a sure sign of whether a person was guilty or not. The pin was inserted into parts of the body and if the wound did not bleed that person was declared to be in league with the devil.

A bell-man was sent through the town to let everyone know that any person that had had a complaint made against them for witchcraft were to be tried by the witch-finder. Thirty suspected witches were brought to the town hall and twenty-seven of them were set aside to be tried. One by one they were stripped in front of the crowd of onlookers and pins thrust into different parts of their bodies.

The witch-finder told Lieutenant Colonel Paul Hobson, Deputy Governor of Newcastle, that he could discover a witch by their looks (most 'witches' would have been elderly old crones). One woman must have stood out from the rest because of her appearance. Hobson stated that she could not be guilty but the witch-finder insisted that she should be tried. The woman was stripped to the waist, her clothes pulled over her head. In her fright and shame, it was recorded, that all her blood contracted into one part of her body. (A severe blush or

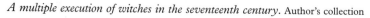

A multiple execution of witches in the seventeenth century. Author's collection

flush would probably have occurred). The witch-finder thrust a pin into her thigh and then let her clothes fall. He then asked why she did not bleed. The terrified woman did not reply. The witch-finder then pulled up her clothes, pulled out the pin and declared her guilty. Hobson watched the woman and as her blood (or flush) settled he demanded that she be tried again. The woman's clothes were lifted to her thigh and the pin inserted into the same place, blood gushed out and the woman was declared not to be a child of the devil.

Out of those tried, fourteen were declared witches and one man a wizard. These unfortunates were all hanged on the Town Moor. In the register of St Andrew's parochial chapelry in Newcastle dated 21 August 1650 the following extract was recorded:

Thes partes her under named wer executed on the town mor for wiches-Mathew Boumer, Isabell Brown, Margrit Maddison, Ann Watson, Ellenor Henderson, Ellenor Rogers, Elsabeth Dobson, Mrs Elsabeth Anderson, Jane Hunter, Jane Koupling, Margrit Brown, Margrit Moffit, Kattren Welsh, Aylles Hume and Mary Pootes.

Also recorded in the register as being executed the same day were: 'Jane Martin the millar's wif of Chattin, for a wich.' Then nine others (described as moss troopers) for stealing:

Ellenor Robson the 21 day stellin of silver spoons, John Ridley, Simend Armstrong, George Armstrong, ? Ellot,, William Brown, ? Johnson, John Armestron, Jo Dronweth,

The Gateshead parish books of 1649 also have an extract which reads: 'Paid at Mris Watson's, when the justices sate to examine the witches 3s 4d; for a grave for a witch 6d, for trying the witches £1.5s.'

The witch-finder had made a small fortune and the magistrates thought that Newcastle was a safer place. On leaving Newcastle the witch-finder went to Northumberland where he received £3 per head for each witch. His reputation must have gone before him so his fee went up. Some people

A sketch by Robert JS Bertram of St Andrew's Church in 1914. It was here that the executed witches were buried in unmarked graves and their names recorded in the parish register. Author's collection

must have had the sense not to believe in witchcraft and one man, Henry Ogle, a Justice of the Peace, questioned what this so-called witch-finder was doing. The witch-finder managed to escape back to Scotland. He had caused the condemnation of witches in Scotland also. Eventually he was arrested and imprisoned. He was tried for the villainy he had carried out in Scotland and executed. On the gallows the witch-finder confessed to having sent 222 women and men in England and Scotland to their deaths for the sum of at least twenty shillings each.

Because of a lack of understanding of even the most basic things, superstition was heavily relied on, not just within the lower classes but throughout all walks of life. Now, if one does not get on with, or has problems with a neighbour either it must be dealt with by the law or put up with. Up until the early eighteenth century one could denounce that neighbour as a witch and quite probably get rid of them forever. Ignorance seemed to have produced a type of mass hysteria and all over Britain witch hunts took place. The witch-finder who caused the deaths of fifteen people in Newcastle was eventually punished by execution but what about the accusers, the magistrates and others involved in the persecution of the wretched souls that were stripped of any dignity and then hanged on the Town Moor? Their only punishment would perhaps have been a feeling of guilt.

Newgate Gaol in 1813. It was here that the witches would have been held whilst awaiting their execution. The gaol was built in the fifteenth century and was used until its demolition in 1823. Author's collection

CHAPTER 2

Murder or Suicide?
1764

D r James Oliphant, who was an apothecary and surgeon, and his wife Margaret, lived on the south-west side of the Tyne Bridge. Dr Oliphant had moved from Perth in Scotland to Gateshead in 1754. Here he met Margaret Erskine and they were married in 1755. They later had two children, William James and Lawrence Thomas. Dr William Erskine, Margaret's father, lived with the couple along with two female domestics, Mary Shittleton and Dinah Armstrong.

Many houses and shops were built on the old Tyne Bridge, one reason being perhaps that it gave easy access to the river for the collecting and shipping of goods.

Mr and Mrs Oliphant went on a month-long visit to Scotland leaving their two children in the care of a friend, Mrs Milne, and one of their servants, Dinah Armstrong. On the Oliphant's return Mrs Milne told them that she suspected Dinah of pilfering several trifling articles from her house, including some damask napkins. Mrs Milne asked Mrs Oliphant to question the girl. Accordingly, this was done and Dinah's possessions were searched. Some articles, including a sheet, belonging to Dinah's previous employer were found. Dinah confessed to having stolen from a former employer but she adamantly denied taking anything from Mrs Milne. She was threatened with prosecution by Mrs Milne, but, for the time being Dinah apparently carried on with her duties for the family until the afternoon of Tuesday, 17 July when she disappeared.

Dinah's body was found on Sunday, 22 July two miles or so above the bridge by two keelmen, one of whom was Joseph Barlow. The body was taken to Dunston to be examined by a doctor. Tied tightly around Dinah's neck was the string of her

The Old Tyne Bridge.

The Old Tyne Bridge on which the Oliphant family lived. Author's collection

The Old Tyne Bridge and the houses that were built upon it being swept away in the flood of 16 November 1771, from an oil painting by Wilson Hepple, Shipley Gallery. Author's collection

bonnet, which made the doctor suspect that she may have been strangled or hanged.

At the inquest Mary Shittleton stated that on Tuesday, 17 July, while the family was at lunch, she noticed that the door from the cellar, which was only a few feet from the river, was open. When she looked out she said she saw Dinah lying on the sand beneath. The family was summoned but when they arrived there was no sign of anyone. Mary said she assumed Dinah had got up and run away

Dr Oliphant was asked to go to Dunston to attend the inquest to justify himself against any part he may have played in the girl's death. On the way to Dunston he was met by an angry mob accusing him of murdering his servant. Dinah's two sisters, Jane and Tamar, had been adding fuel to the rumours and had branded Dr Oliphant as a 'murdering dog'.

Mr Robson, the coroner for the county of Durham, had the parish constable arrest Mr and Mrs Oliphant and Mary

Robert Mylne's Tyne Bridge was constructed to replace the first bridge that was destroyed by floods. This bridge was demolished in 1866. In the background are the Moot Hall, St Nicholas' Church and the Castle Keep. Author's collection

Shittleton for wilful murder. It was said he was influenced by the prejudices of an infatuated rabble. Mr Robson did not hold his suspects in gaol but allowed them to return home in the custody of the local constable. The family returned to Durham on 13 August to stand trial before Justice Bathurst for strangling Dinah and throwing her body into the river.

Witnesses came forward as to the good character of the family and eventually Justice Bathurst stated they had been arrested without a shred of evidence against them. There was no real evidence that Dinah had been strangled. They were a reputable and worthy family of unblemished and respectable character and there had been a violation of the dearest rights of man. They were found not guilty and allowed to leave the court.

Dr Oliphant would have taken action for libel against the coroner but did not have the funds to do so. In 1768 he wrote a book on the events that had taken place in a bid to put his story to the public. The family was again visiting Scotland

ST. MARYS CHURCH: GATESHEAD.

A sketch by Robert Bertram of St Mary's Church in Gateshead in 1914. The Oliphant family moved to Church Gare when their Tyne Bridge home was destroyed. Author's collection

when the Great Flood of 1771 destroyed their home. On their return they stayed in Church Gare, Gateshead for a short time before returning to Scotland to live. Dr Oliphant died in 1791.

It was said by some at the time that Dinah was 'weak minded.' Was she perhaps of simple intellect and in her fear of being arrested commited suicide? As she jumped from the cellar to the river bed below did her bonnet fly back and the string catch around her neck? If this was so, how did she get from where she fell into the river two miles upstream? Unless she was only stunned by her fall and did indeed run away as Mary suggested and then later, in a confused state, she stumbled into the river and drowned. Did Mary Shittleton strangle Dinah and then push her from the cellar? If that were the case then how did Mary get Dinah's body into the river? Was Mary telling the truth about seeing Dinah lying on the sand? No one else saw her. Or was this a conspiracy by the whole family to murder Dinah and then cover it up, but for what reason? If the family were really angry about the thefts then surely they could have called the local constable and had the girl arrested. According to the family's statements they allowed Dinah to carry on her domestic duties as if nothing had happened. It seems that there was either not enough evidence for them to convict the girl or they were a forgiving family who decided to give Dinah another chance. Then why would she commit suicide!

CHAPTER 3

The Demon Drink
1752–1901

3.1 Bigg Market, 1752:

On 23 May some company went into Mr Pinkney's public house in the Bigg market. Words took place between the company and nineteen-year old Ewen MacDonald, a recruit in General Guise's regiment of Highlanders. It may have been because MacDonald was wearing a kilt and the locals were poking fun at him. MacDonald must have come to the end of his tether and he began fighting with a cooper named Parker. Some of the company left but MacDonald followed them and took hold of Robert Parker, also a cooper and possibly the brother of the first of MacDonald's victims. MacDonald viciously stabbed Parker in the back of the neck. He then re-entered the public house and caused havoc with the locals, breaking a man's arm in the process. He was finally subdued and taken to Newgate by a file of musqueteers.

MacDonald was found guilty of murder and sentenced to be executed on 28 September. Before his execution he expressed sorrow for what he had done. The general feeling towards the man was pity as it was felt that he had been grossly provoked. As MacDonald reached the gallows on the Town Moor at Newcastle his behavior again became violent as he tried to throw John Young, the executioner, off the ladder. He was eventually sent to meet his maker and his body was taken to the surgeon's hall. Later records stated that as the body was being placed ready for dissection, the surgeons were called to attend a case at the infirmary. On their return MacDonald was very much alive, sitting up and begging for mercy. A young surgeon, not wishing to be deprived from performing a dissection, picked up a heavy wooden mallet and killed MacDonald. It was later reported, that in just revenge

The Barber Surgeons' Hall in 1830. The hall was rebuilt in 1730 and was used for the dissection of bodies for medical research and lectures on the findings. Ewen MacDonald was the first executed criminal to have his body disposed of in this way under The Murder Act of 1752. Author's collection

the young surgeon was killed shortly afterwards in his stable by his own horse. Perhaps it was Ewen MacDonald's ghost that wreaked the vengeance!

A new act called *The Murder Act of 1752* allowed the bodies of executed prisoners to be given to the surgeons for dissection and anatomical lectures. This was partly to discourage the body snatchers and partly to deter a would-be criminal by making his fate as degrading as possible. MacDonald was the first executed prisoner to be treated this way under the new legislation.

3.2 Benwell, 1786:
Mrs Sparke had kept the *Black Bull* alehouse in the Flesh Market at Newcastle before she moved to Benwell. On the evening of 24 November Mrs Sparke's son, after spending

some time drinking with his mother in her upstairs apartment, came downstairs very drunk. Sparke spoke to the servant girl telling her he was going to kill the cat. He then caught hold of the poor creature and bashed its brains out. Sparke then pushed the servant out of the front door and locked it from the inside. She spent the night at a neighbouring house and returned to the Sparke's house the following morning. The door was open and when the servant entered Sparke told her he had been fighting with the devil all night. He then said the devil had been dressed in his mother's clothes and was now

The Flesh Market in 1832 where Mrs Sparke had once kept the Black Bull *alehouse.* Author's collection

lying dead upstairs. At first the servant took no notice because Sparke had often said strange things and at times seemed not quite sane. After a time, when her mistress had not appeared, the servant became concerned. On going upstairs she found Mrs Sparke lying on the bed with a multitude of wounds to her body. The bedclothes were scattered all over the room and were covered in blood. On examination of the body, besides the many wounds, the neck was found to be discoloured and swollen.

Sparke stood trial at the Assizes for wilful murder in August 1787. The jury's verdict was that having been intoxicated for some days it had produced delirium, which had resulted in perfect insanity. Sparke was then acquitted. This case is one of many that showed the low esteem that women were held in.

3.3 Elford, 1790:

Thomas Watson was a single man living with his father who had a farm at Elford. George Gibson was married and lived at a farm at Coldrife near Newham in Northumberland. The two men had been intimate friends until Gibson accused Watson of an unnatural crime. Watson became very angry and swore he would kill Gibson. On 5 August he purchased a pistol, powder and balls from a gunsmith in Alnwick. Watson then went and got himself drunk and lay in wait for Gibson at a place he expected his unsuspecting victim to pass. Gibson did not appear, so, the following morning Watson went to Gibson's farm and shot him through the heart. Gibson died instantly.

At Watson's trial an attempt was made to prove temporary insanity but this could not be substantiated. When the death sentence was pronounced Watson showed no emotion. He was executed on a temporary gallows outside Westgate and his body given to the surgeons for dissection.

During Watson's trial a young woman called Jane Stephenson was caught stealing a handkerchief from a young man's pocket. She was immediately secured, tried and sentenced to seven years transportation. All this took place within a matter of minutes.

3.4 The Town Moor, 1795:

On Race Sunday, on the evening of 21 June, Thomas Purvis, a carver and gilder, was in company of some friends in a tent on the Town Moor. Some pitmen who were there quarreled with the landlord and refused to pay for the liquor they had drunk. Purvis interfered telling the pitmen to pay the landlord what they owed. After a few words the men paid up and left. Ten minutes or so went by and the pitmen returned with six or seven more men in tow. They began making threats, especially towards Purvis. John Wallis, a constable, managed to quieten the situation and the men left, but not before telling Purvis that they would lay in wait for him.

Later that night when Purvis left the tent the men were waiting for him. They were beating and kicking him mercilessly when two men passing by interrupted them. The men ran off leaving their victim lying on the ground bleeding from his many wounds. Purvis died, in terrible agony, of his injuries the following Sunday.

Westgate in the early nineteenth century. It was here that Thomas Watson was executed. It was also the site of many of the early public executions. The last execution to be held here was in 1805. Author's collection

Five men were arrested in connection with the murder. Henry Turnbull and Thomas Maddox gave evidence for the crown so were allowed to go free. Francis Grey, Thomas Nicholson and John Nicholson, who were brothers, went on trial for murder. Thomas Nicholson, who was twenty-three, was found guilty and hanged on the Town Moor on Saturday, 8 August. The other two men were acquitted.

Purvis had been a musician in the Gentlemen Volunteers of Newcastle. The corps set up a subscription for his widow and children.

3.5 Newcastle, 1829:

Jane Jameson hawked fish and other commodities. She was known as a disgusting creature of very masculine appearance and was generally under the influence of drink. It was said that she had once, in a drunken rage, tried to cut her father's

The Keelmen's Hospital on the Quayside in 1843. The keelmen carried coal from the quay to the colliers downstream. Because there was little medical help for the poor the hospital was built by the keelmen in 1701 by the levy of a penny on every keel carried. Besides being in use as a hospital there were also dwelling rooms for keelmen's widows. Jane Jameson's mother occupied one of the rooms. Author's collection

throat. She visited her mother, Margaret, who was an inmate of the Keelman's Hospital, quite regularly. Margaret liked a drop or two of rum herself and, according to neighbours, the pair would sometimes argue and throw things at on another, although Jane had never been seen to strike the elderly lady.

On 2 January Jane visited Margaret. Neighbours later stated that Jane was very drunk and the pair had words with Jane accusing her mother of killing a man (probably referring to Margaret's husband). Margaret shouted back that she had never killed anyone but Jane had murdered her two bairns. Margaret was then heard to cry out as if in pain. When a neighbour entered the room to see what was wrong she found Margaret sitting on the floor bleeding from a wound to her chest. The wound had been inflicted with a poker which was lying on the floor nearby. Margaret lingered on until 11

A sketch of Jane Jameson as she appeared at her trial. Author's collection

January. She insisted to the end that she had fallen on the poker and that her daughter was not responsible for the injury.

At Jane's trial, on 5 March, there was conflicting evidence from Jane and from friends and neighbours. Medical opinion was that the wound had been inflicted with great force but it could not be said for certain whether Margaret had indeed fallen on the poker or Jane had used it as a weapon. The jury found Jane guilty of murder and she received the death sentence. While in gaol waiting for Judgment Day the prison

This photograph shows the bell tower of St Andrew's Church on Newgate Street in 2003. The church is believed to be the oldest in Newcastle. Although much altered since its beginnings, it originally dates from the 12th century. The author

chaplain, Reverend Robert Green, visited Jane. He begged her to confess and unburden her soul. She replied:

I might as well say that I had done it, as that I had not done it, for I was so drunk that I knew nothing at all about it. I am resigned to my fate but lament being hanged like a dog.

At Jane's hanging, on 7 March, it was estimated there were 20,000 spectators. More than half were female. Pick-pocketing in the crowd was rife. As well as the on-lookers near to the gallows, people were watching from every window along the route that the procession took. Jane was the first female to be hanged at Newcastle for over seventy years.

Her body was left to hang for an hour, as was the custom. At eleven in the morning she was cut down and taken to the ground floor of the surgeon's hall. Here the body was left on display to the public until six that evening. Afterwards the

The gates of Newcastle gaol. It was here that Jane Jameson was incarcerated while awaiting her trial and subsequent sentence. The building was situated on Carliol Square. Erection of the gaol began in 1823 and was completed in 1828. The gaol was demolished about 1929 and some of the stone was used in the erection of the King George V Bridge. Author's collection

body was given to the surgeons for dissection and anatomical lectures.

The trial had taken eight hours and the expenses for the execution consisted of payment for cart and driver, joiner, porters, servants, constables, executioner, horses, mourning coach, halter and cord and for tolling St Andrew's bell. The total came to £28 13s 3d. (£28.66)

3.6 Death in the Tyne, 1834:

A trial was held on Saturday, 2 August before Lord Lyndhurst at the Guildhall in Newcastle into the death of a seaman, Thomas Lee. On 22 July several seamen, including Lee, and a group of pitmen had been at a dance at a house at Hebburn Quay on the south side of the river Tyne, about six miles east of Newcastle. During the course of the evening a few quarrels had broken out among those in attendance but most had just fizzled out. Lee and a pitman, William Willis, were two of the men that had been arguing.

A view of Newcastle about 1900 showing the Guildhall in the foreground, where William Willis was tried for the murder of Thomas Lee in 1834. Author's collection

On the morning of 23 July Lee left the house followed by Willis and his wife. Lee's body was found in the Tyne shortly afterwards. There were marks of violence on his body believed to have been caused by a fist. Willis, who was twenty-three, was charged with Lee's murder. At the trial Willis was found guilty of manslaughter by seizing Lee around the body and throwing him into the river. Willis was sentenced to seven years transportation.

3.7 The Glass House, 1836:

Lee (no first name provided in the records) was, according to the local papers at the time, a defenceless young man who became the victim of a cold blooded and atrocious murder. Lee lived in Gallowgate, Newcastle and was a member of the Northumberland and Newcastle yeomanry cavalry.

On the evening of 30 September Lee had consumed a considerable amount of alcohol at a public house in Pipwellgate. He escorted a female acquaintance to her door before setting off to his own home. Lee proceeded, walking with great difficulty, towards the glass house. He often visited three of his friends there, Thomas Errington and Thomas

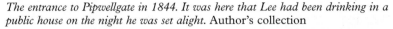

The entrance to Pipwellgate in 1844. It was here that Lee had been drinking in a public house on the night he was set alight. Author's collection

Wardman who were both nineteen and Henry Brown who was eighteen. The previous evening he had been out drinking with Brown and there had been no ill will between them.

Lee must have managed to walk as far as the glass house and decided he could go no further. He entered and lying down on a large box, fell into a deep sleep. The three so-called friends then hatched a plot that one must assume was supposed to be a joke. Errington brought a straw rope from the door and loosened both ends. He then stuffed one end into Lee's shirt at the chest and left the other end trailing on the floor. All three then collected some loose straw that was lying about and placed it on the floor at the end of the straw rope. Errington then went to the furnace with a shovel and filled it with burning cinders and then ignited the pile of straw, which flared up and then died down again without touching the sleeping man. Lee awoke and muttered something and then immediately went back to asleep. A boy named Dykes was witness to these acts and he tried to wake Lee to warn him of what was taking place. Errington thrust Dykes out of the way and threatened him with death if he interfered again. He then took the shovel back to the furnace and filled it once again with burning cinders. Again the straw flared up but without the fire touching Lee. Errington then gathered up some of the burning straw and threw it on Lee's chest. The three perpetrators followed by Dykes all ran out. However, curiosity took hold of them and they headed back in to see what was happening. They were met on the way in by Lee who was enveloped in flames and crying 'fire'. The burning man ran along the street where his cries were heard by a neighbour, Mary Thompson, who tried to reach Lee to give him assistance. Lee in his pain and confusion ran down an alley and then back again. As he came out of the alley, Mary Thompson and John Brown, Henry Brown's brother, managed to get hold of Lee and put out the fire. They took him to an entry where a Mrs Linley came down from the house above and dressed his wounds as best she could. The injured man was then taken to the house of Mr Grant where they prepared to take him to the infirmary. Errington was in his mother's house at this time and told her that he was going

Newcastle Infirmary in 1803. Author's collection

to help to carry Lee to the infirmary. This he did along with four or five others.

Lee was severely burnt on the thighs, arms and belly and it was known that recovery was impossible. It was recorded that he was in a deep depression but it was likely that he was actually in a coma. Stimulants were given to try to revive the young man but to no avail. Everything that could be done for him was done but there was no improvement. About twenty-four hours after the fire was started, Lee died. The three men involved had already been arrested and now the charge was murder.

At the Assizes in February of 1837 the three men were convicted of manslaughter. Errington was sentenced to ten years transportation and Brown and Wardman to two years imprisonment with hard labour.

Lee was buried in St Andrew's churchyard with full military honours. Even though it was a dull, winter's day, huge crowds assembled in the streets to watch the funeral procession.

St Andrew's Churchyard in 2003. It was here that Lee was buried with full military honours. The author

3.8 Newbrough, 1847:

Situated about five miles west of Hexham, the quiet little village of Newbrough was shaken to its core by a senseless murder. Thomas Proud, who worked as a hand to Mr Maughan of Newbrough Lodge, had his child christened on 7 February. After the service the men went to Mr Surtees' public house. One of the guests was a young man named James Welch who was a labourer at Prudolm Quarry. The drink flowed, but, instead of a celebration the day turned into a catastrophe. Welch and Proud began quarrelling and the situation turned nasty. Everyone left the public house to return to their homes. Welch, however, must have been harbouring a grudge. He followed Proud and on catching up with him, slit his throat with a clasp knife.

Welch was apprehended a little later at Fourstones and, on 26 February, was tried before Baron Rolfe and found guilty of murder. His execution was carried out at Morpeth on 26 March.

3.9 North Shields, 1868:

In December of 1869 James Hayes, a twenty-five-year-old American sailor, was indicted for the manslaughter of George Kaiser at North Shields on 24 August 1868.

Samuel Arrowsmith, landlord of the *Black Lion Inn*, Clive Street, said that the two men had been at the inn on the day of the fatality. Hayes was bouncing about saying what he had done in America. Suddenly, without warning, Hayes struck Kaiser in the face. As far as Arrowsmith could see there was no reason for his behaviour. Kaiser took hold of Hayes by the neck to restrain him but did not strike him back. The landlord called PC Brown who ejected the two men from the inn. Both men

Low Street in North Shields in 1843.
Author's collection

returned a few minutes later to collect their caps, which they had left behind. Hayes then went to leave with Kaiser behind him. As Hayes reached the door, he turned and struck Kaiser a second blow to the face. A man by the name of Casely was on the New Quay that day and had seen the two men just after they had left the inn for the second time. He heard one of the men say 'You cowardly son of a bitch, if you use a knife I'll whip you.' Kaiser was unbuttoning his coat when the two men went into a clinch and Casely heard one of the men shout that he had been stabbed. Hayes had stabbed Kaiser twice, once in the chest and once in the lower part of his bowel. Hayes entrails were protruding from his body.

PC Brown had been nearby and approached just as the stabbing took place. He took hold of Hayes to take him to the police station but his prisoner struck him and managed to get away. PC Brown went after Hayes and used his staff in consequence of the prisoner's violence. This time Hayes was restrained and escorted to the police station. Kaiser was taken to the workhouse at Tynemouth but died soon after from inflammation of the bowel caused by the wound he had received.

On the jury bringing in a verdict of guilty, Justice Lush, in his closing statement, said that even though this was only a moment of drunkenness, there was no excuse for the violence that had been used against a defenceless man. He sentenced Hayes to life in penal servitude.

3.10 Barrack Road, 1901:
On Saturday, 9 November 1901 a night out in Newcastle ended with a pointless argument and, ultimately, a fatality.

In the early hours of Sunday morning, a lamp-lighter, named Vincent, was making his way up Barrack Street when he saw a man lying with his back against a tramway pole. It was raining heavily and as Vincent approached he could see the man, who seemed to be unconscious, was soaking wet and covered in mud. Vincent went for the police and they in turn called an ambulance. The man was taken to Newcastle Infirmary where he was attended to by the house surgeon, Dr Froggat. The doctor found that the man had a wound on the right side of the head and a black eye. On regaining consciousness the man said his name was Robert Hackney. As the day went on Hackney's condition became worse. He became restless and had to be strapped down. By Monday paralysis had set in to his left leg and arm so it was decided to operate to see if there was pressure on the brain. It was thought that Hackney had a fractured skull but no pressure could be found. He gradually weakened and died on Tuesday morning. A post-mortem found the cause of death was indeed a fractured skull, probably caused by a fall. On these findings the coroner ordered a police investigation to be carried out.

Edward Adams Addison of 34 Bell Street had met Hackney at the *Windsor Hotel* at 8.30 on Saturday night where they had a glass of beer together. Addison then went into another room leaving Hackney at the bar. Addison and another man, John Cosser of 41 Hindhaugh Street, had left at about 11 pm. As they were leaving they had seen Hackney tumble backwards over the step on the pavement outside the hotel. There were five or six men standing about at the time. Addison did not see

Newcastle Infirmary in 1827. It was here that Robert Hackney was taken after being found in the street by a lamp-lighter. Author's collection

High Street, Gateshead in 1844. Author's collection

the events leading up to this but Cosser saw Hackney and another man arguing and then what looked like a punch to Hackney's face which caused him to fall. Neither of the two witnesses could identify the man Hackney was arguing with.

The police then found another witness, George Bowman of Westminster Street, in Gateshead. Bowman had gone with his two brothers, a friend and a man called James Worth to the *Windsor Hotel.* As they were leaving one of Bowman's brothers and Hackney started a heated discussion. Bowman and Worth started to walk away but then Worth went back and began arguing with Hackney. The argument was about the English and the Scots. Hackney seemed to be winding Worth up about his origin and said that he was not an Englishman. Worth became angry and said he was an Englishman as he had fought for his country. He then hit Hackney who fell backwards. The men left him lying on the pavement and went home.

In the early hours of Sunday morning, William Surtees, a barman at the *Adelaide Hotel* in Newgate Street was walking up Barrack Road on his way home when he saw a man, who appeared to be very drunk, being held up against a wall by two other men. These good Samaritans were trying to get the 'drunken' man to speak and tell them where he lived. Surtees went to Mrs Dalrymple at 15 Barrack Road to ask if the man could lie in her passage as he was drunk and it was raining very heavily outside. The good lady consented and Hackney was brought in and laid in the passage out of the rain. Mrs Dalrymple gave him a drink of water and she and her husband tried to rouse the man but to no avail. A policeman passed and was called in but said as the man was drunk they should just let him lie there. A little later Hackney awoke and with the aid of Mr Dalrymple made it out into the street. That was the last time the couple saw him. Hackney was then found by the lamplighter and taken to the infirmary where he later died.

All the men that were there that night insisted that although they had been drinking from about 8.30 until 11pm they were all, including Worth, stone-cold sober. To the jury at the trial it did not matter if the men were drunk or sober. They concluded that whether it had been the blow that was delivered or the subsequent fall, Worth had caused Hackney's death and he was found guilty of manslaughter.

CHAPTER 4

The Faw Gang
1791

Margaret Crozier was an elderly woman who occupied a part of the old Pele House at the Raw near Elsdon. She kept a small shop in the house where she sold drapery. On Monday, 29 August 1791 Mary Temple, a fine needlewoman, and Elizabeth Jackson, who was the daughter of the farmer of Pele House, stopped by for a chat with Margaret before bedtime. After an hour or so of conversation the two young women took their leave. As they did so they heard dogs barking around a pike of hay that was only a short distance from the house. They instructed Margaret to remember to bolt her door to which she laughingly replied she had nothing to fear. On the following morning a neighbour, Barbara Drummond, called to purchase some commodity from Margaret. On reaching the house she noticed some thread near the front door. Barbara went to Elizabeth Jackson and William Dodds, a joiner, to tell them she thought something was peculiar. Margaret was usually out and about by this time but no one had seen her so the three neighbours went to Margaret's house. The front door was not bolted so they entered. Margaret's body was on the bed. Her throat had been cut and around her face and neck was a handkerchief tied very tightly.

The Pele House as it looked in 1791, where Margaret Crozier was robbed and murdered. The Pele at Raw still stands, now incorporated into farm buildings. Author's collection

One of her hands was badly lacerated and in the bed was a gully knife stained with blood. It was obvious that the old lady had fought hard with her assailant, the cut on her hand would have happened when she tried to ward off her attacker. The cut on her throat was not deep enough to have caused death so it seemed that the handkerchief had caused Margaret to suffocate. Outside was a plough coulter that had been used to force the door open. There were also some rather distinctive footprints that had been made with hobnailed boots. Drapery, handkerchiefs, muslin, printed cottons and other articles were missing so it seemed the motive had been robbery.

The people of the neighbourhood, especially the higher classes, rallied round to try and detect the murderer. Many were familiar with the goods that Margaret sold and a detailed inventory was taken of the articles known to be missing. The officers of the parish of Elsdon offered a reward of £5 leading to the conviction of the offender.

It transpired that on the day preceding the murder, two boys had seen a man and two women near a sheep fold above the Whitlees farm house. They were sitting eating a piece of fat mutton and bread while their ass grazed nearby. One of the boys, Robert Hindmarsh, from the Whiskerfield farm, had noticed the man using a gully knife to cut the meat. Hindmarsh was close enough to also see the man's feet and notice some rather unusual nails that were on the sole and heel of his shoes. The boys told William Marshall of Landshott what they had seen and he in turn told the coroner. The coroner had the boys brought before him and Hindmarsh said that the gully knife found in Margaret's bed was the same type that the stranger had been using to cut the mutton. He also thought that the shoes he had seen on the man's feet matched footprints that were found outside Pele House. Others had noticed the three strangers in the vicinity on the same day the boys had seen them. The following day the same three had been seen driving a loaded ass to Harlow Hill.

Three constables, John Brown of Laing's Hill, William Hall of Elsdon and William Tweedy of Hudspeth, went in pursuit of the suspects. Near Horsley they came upon a man fitting the description of the suspect and he was duly arrested. The

Newgate Street in Morpeth in the nineteenth century. Jane Clark and William Winter were held in Morpeth gaol to await their initial trial. Author's collection

constables then went in search of the women. A woman accompanied by a dog was arrested a couple of miles west of Ovingham. The two prisoners at first denied knowing each other but the dog, by its actions, obviously knew the man and it was soon discovered that the prisoners were both members of a Faw Gang (wandering groups that roamed the country begging and stealing). The man, who was in his early twenties, was William Winter. He had just been released after a term in gaol for theft. His father and brother had both been executed at Morpeth the previous year. The woman was Jane Clarke the younger, alias Jane Douglass, who in the winter season usually resided at Hedley Fell near Ryton in Durham.

The two prisoners were taken to Mitford to be examined by B Mitford who had the authority of a Justice of the Peace. On

Winter being stripped, bloodstains were found on his shirt which, he said, had happened in a fight with one of his gang. It was decided that if Williams had been in a fight he would have removed his shirt as Gypsies always fought bare-chested so his account of the bloodstains was ruled out. On 3 September the two were committed to the county gaol at Morpeth. Meanwhile, the search had continued for the second woman. She was apprehended along with another woman at Barley Moor in Tynedale. The woman that had been seen with the two prisoners was Eleanor Clarke alias Eleanor Douglass. The other woman was Jane Clarke the elder, alias Jane Douglass, and alias Jane Gregg. On 14 September these two women were also committed to Morpeth gaol. The Assizes

The old Moot Hall in Castle Garth in 1809 where the trial of the Faw Gang was held. This sketch was done just before the hall was pulled down to make way for the new County Courts. The back wall was so thick it was believed that it was probably part of the original Roman wall. Author's collection

were, at this time, only held once a year in August so there was plenty of time in which to collect evidence before the trial. The three prisoners were held in solitary confinement for eleven months. Eventually, early in the month of August of 1792, the trial took place in the Moot Hall at Newcastle.

It came to light that in July of 1791 Margaret had received a quantity of drapery goods that she had purchased and was showing them to Elizabeth Jackson. Jane Clarke the elder had entered the house and looked at the goods on display and then left. Margaret had commented to Elizabeth that 'she did not like the appearance of that woman – she gazed so much about her'. It was said that Jane exerted herself to having the younger members of her family 'put forth their hands and steal.' If it was mentioned to her that a situation may be dangerous she would say 'what's five minutes hanging to a year's pleasure.' With the evidence that was produced the conclusion was that the elder Jane had been the chief instigator of the robbery and murder of Margaret. Her two daughters were about twenty. A nightcap and apron that were found in the possession of Jane Clarke the younger and Eleanor Clarke were identified as having belonged to Margaret. The strongest evidence was that of Robert Hindmarsh, who at the time of the trial was about eleven years of age. Winter, knowing he was in deep trouble, confessed to the robbery. He stated that when he left the house after stealing the goods the old woman was still alive but he had sent the two women back to make sure that the neighbours had not been alerted. The women had told him that they 'had tied her up from the meat', a saying meaning to tie up a horse by the bridle or halter so that it cannot eat.

At the end of a sixteen-hour trial the elder Jane Clarke was released but the other three were found guilty of Margaret's murder and their executions were ordered.

On Friday, 10 August 1792 the prisoners were placed on a cart and conveyed through the Westgate. Beyond the ancient portal, almost on the spot where a watercourse formed on the east side of the *Waterloo Inn*, a gallows was erected. The executioner was William Gardner who had been convicted of sheep stealing and sentenced to death. Gardner's sentence was changed to transportation when he agreed to carry out the

The Castle Keep in the eighteenth century. It was here that the Faw gang would have been imprisoned after their trial while awaiting their executions. Author's collection

triple execution. Before they were hanged, Winter admitted his guilt and went to the gallows with no apparent fear. The two women protested their innocence until the end. The bodies of the women were given to the surgeons for dissection. Winter's body was gibbeted at Steng Cross within sight of the Raw. Thousands came to see the grisly spectacle. The body hung there until the smell became so bad that horses would shy away as they passed. When the bones began to come apart they were hung up in a new sack which was tarred inside and out to preserve it. When the bones began to drop once again the shepherds would bury them. A crude wooden figure was then erected with Winter's skull on the top. Eventually, this too decayed and it was said that the skull was conveyed to the owner of some landed property near the Barracks at Newcastle.

The boy, Richard Hindmarsh, after giving his testimony was thought to be in danger of revenge by the Faws. Mr Trevelyan of Netherwitton took him into his protection. He remained as a servant to Mr Trevelyan for several years before going to live with Rev Mr Johnson of Bywell to further his education. Still considered to be in danger, Hindmarsh was moved to the residence of Colonel Baird who lived north of Aberdeen. Here the young man became ill and was sent home. He sailed to Berwick and then went by carriage to his father's home at Whiskerfield. Hindmarsh died there in September 1803 at the age of twenty-two.

Today, at Steng Cross on the Northumberland Moors, there stands a replica gibbet with a wooden head swinging from it, a sordid reminder of past punishments and a tourist attraction for the morbidly curious.

On 14 August 1793, Margaret Dunn and Walter Clarke were executed at Fair Moor, Morpeth. Dunn was found guilty of stealing cash and clothing from a house in Corbridge. When she was caught she was wearing apparel from the house. Clark was found guilty of burglary. He was the father of Eleanor and Jane, the two sisters who were executed with William Winter in 1792.

The entrance to the Port of Berwick where Richard Hindmarsh sailed from to go into hiding. Author's collection

CHAPTER 5

Guilty on the Word of a Felon
1809

ear to Ponteland there was a large farming estate known as Kirtley Hall. The estate was owned by Nathaniel Ogle. As on most estates where there were tenant farmers the rents were collected twice yearly. Ogle was often absent from Kirtley Hall as he owned other estates in various areas. Michael Aynsley, who was a smaller landowner at nearby Newham, would take care of Ogle's affairs while he was away. When the spring rents were due Aynsley collected them. The total amount came to over £1000, a considerable amount of money in 1809. Aynsley hid the money in a wooden chest behind a secret panel in the house. He went home to his own estate and sent a letter to Ogle telling him that the rents had been collected and hidden in the place they had agreed upon.

The following morning Aynsley returned to Kirtley Hall to attend to other business that he had agreed to carry out for Ogle to find that the house had been

The Castle Keep in the late nineteenth century. James Charlton was held here in 1809 on suspicion of stealing. The author

broken into and the money stolen. When Ogle was contacted about the theft he asked Detective Lavender of London to investigate. On Lavender instigating a search of the property most of the money was found in the garden. Lavender then made enquiries as to who else knew of the hiding place behind the panel. Suspicion immediately fell on James Charlton. He had been employed on the estate for about four years as a handyman. Charlton had a reputation for being honest and hardworking. He had a wife and four children, was very poor, in debt and knew of the hiding place. When Lavender started questioning the local people he was told that just after the theft Charlton had paid most of his debts and was in the local pub offering to buy drinks for his friends. Charlton was arrested in May and taken to the Newcastle Keep where he was held in chains until the next Assizes.

At the Assizes held in August Aynsley, as an upstanding member of the community, was the prosecutor in the case. Charlton protested his innocence saying that the money he had was borrowed from his brother. Charlton's brother confirmed the statement. Charlton went on to accuse Aynsley of the theft bringing in witnesses who said that Aynsley had been nervous when the detective arrived. Charlton also said that Aynsley had known about the borrowed money and had carried out the theft with the intention of the blame being laid on Charlton. Dorothy Hodgson, a servant at Kirtley Hall told the court that when they were discussing the theft, Aynsley had told her that the money would turn up and of course most of it had. Charlton was cleared and released.

While Charlton was held in the Newcastle Keep a fellow inmate was William Taylerson who was in prison for horse stealing, a crime punishable with death. Taylerson was well known within the criminal justice system as a liar and thief. When he heard of Charlton's release he asked the guards if he could avoid the death penalty if he gave evidence against Charlton. Charlton was re-arrested and Taylerson gave evidence that Charlton had told him he had carried out the robbery but would get away with it. This time the jury found Charlton guilty and he was sentenced to life in penal servitude. Taylerson had traded Charlton's life for his own.

The ground floor of the Castle in 1826. Prisoners were held in chains attached to the walls. Author's collection

In our present justice system only the word of a convicted felon would not be enough evidence to find a person guilty. Someone involved in the case would not be allowed to carry out any court duties at all, especially to prosecute or defend a case. Aynsley could certainly have carried out the theft and then became worried when a top detective turned up to investigate so put most of the money in the garden where it could be found. Perhaps Charlton was the guilty party but if he was innocent what chance did a poor servant have against landed gentry?

CHAPTER 6

Was He Guilty?
1816

Charles Stuart was the watchman of the Ouseburn Pottery works near Newcastle. On 4 December 1816 he was attacked and badly beaten before being tied up and his head covered. The premises were then searched and robbed. The following morning Stuart was found barely alive. He was taken to the infirmary where he lingered for about three weeks before succumbing to his injuries. When he was found he named Charles Smith as one of his two attackers. Stuart said that he recognized Smith by his broad Irish accent and his size. He said he did not recognize the second man.

Charles Smith was originally from Sunderland. He had served in the army and had then taken employment at the Fulwell Lime Works. When Stuart died the police were sent to arrest Smith. On a search of his home they found one of his stockings, a boot and breeches supposedly bloodstained. There was also a large bludgeon that appeared to be covered

The Newcastle Infirmary in 1909. It was here that Charles Stuart was taken in 1816 after he had been severely beaten. Author's collection

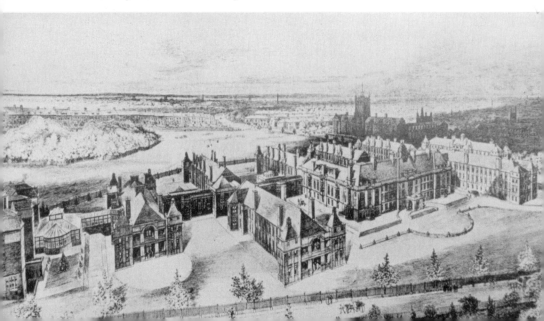

in blood. Smith was charged with the murder of Charles
Stuart. The judge at the trial was concerned with the evidence
of the deceased man and referred the case on a point of law to
twelve judges. There seems to have been some controversy

*The Town Moor where Smith was hanged opposite the cavalry barracks from
Reid's plan of Newcastle 1908.* Author's collection

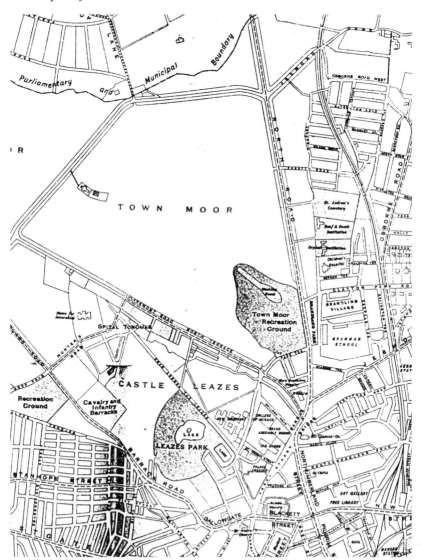

over this and it was a day short of a year before the case was settled and Smith was sentenced to death.

Throughout his trial and the ensuing months waiting for sentence, Smith continuously protested his innocence in any part of the murder and robbery. He stated that he hoped his wife and children would not suffer because he had been found guilty of murder. When he was told he was to be executed for the crime he was asked to name his accomplice. Smith said he had nothing to say but asked that his body would be given to his wife for burial.

A gallows was erected on the Town Moor a little north of the barracks on the opposite side of the road. Forty-nine year old Smith prayed with a Roman Catholic clergyman, Rev Worswick, before the noose was placed around his neck and he was sent to meet his maker on Wednesday, 3 December 1817. As the law of the times allowed his body was then given to the surgeons for dissection. A macabre relic of Smith still remains within the collection of Newcastle City Library in the form of a piece of his skin that was bound into a book detailing his trial.

CHAPTER 7

The Pitmen's Revenge
1832

It is a well known fact that throughout the early history of coal mining the conditions and pay for the pitmen were deplorable and discontent was inevitable. Stands (or strikes) amongst the workers obtained no sympathy from the mine owners, or masters as they were known, and, because there were always others looking for work, often the dissenters would be left unemployed. The houses that the pitmen occupied were owned by their employers so if the workforce was sacked they would also be evicted from their dwellings.

In April of 1832 the stand at Hetton Colliery had caused many of the pitmen to be evicted as their masters had engaged new workers who needed the accommodation. Some of the resident pitmen would not leave their houses so were on the premises illegally. On Saturday, 21 April the long arm of the law was called in to use forcible ejection to remove the men and their families from the houses. Police from the London force assisted by a detachment of the Queen's Bays stood in readiness for any trouble. Those who were not with the strikers were given arms for their protection. All seemed to go peaceably except for a few occasional shots that were fired by the strikers as if to intimidate the new workforce. All day and into late evening furniture and families were brought from the houses and although no resistance was offered the air was electric with tension.

The following morning it was discovered that all had not been as peaceful as thought. John Errington had, at first, stood alongside his comrades in their stand but he had then turned his back on them and consented to be rebound to his masters, becoming what was known as a blackleg. For this he paid with his life. He had been shot and murdered. Even after his death his former co-workers jeered and hissed as his funeral procession passed them.

TC Maynard conducted the inquest into Errington's death and after investigations lasting about ten days four men were brought before the court. George Strong and John Turnbull were charged with wilful murder and John Moore and Luke Hutton as accessories. They were escorted to Durham by an armed cavalry in case their comrades tried to rescue them.

On Tuesday, 1 May evictions were still taking place at several of the collieries in the North-East. Forty-five newly employed lead miners that were on their way through Gateshead to the Tyne Main and Friars' Goose collieries were attacked by those whose places they were taking. Two were nearly killed and many were injured by being pelted with stones. Special constables were appointed and on Wednesday and on Thursday they were at Friars' Goose to complete the evictions. Several hundred pitmen descended on the area firing stones and other missiles at those that were trying to evict the families. Over the next few days all was chaos but eventually the evictions were completed.

Over forty people were arrested and locked up in Newcastle Gaol. About twenty of these, including three women, stood trial at Durham, the others were released.

The sentences on those convicted ranged from being bound over to keep the peace to short terms in prison.

Many years later, in 1849, pit strikes were still taking place and blacklegs were still hated. One incident which occurred on 20 October was the murder of George Hunter. He had refused to join the trade union at Cowpen Colliery. As he was proceeding from Cowpen to Blyth Square he was waylaid by two men and bludgeoned to death. The perpetrators were never caught.

Newcastle Gaol in 1826. Those involved in the affray during the evictions of the miners were locked up here. Author's collection

CHAPTER 8

A Violent Robbery
1833

Illiam Buddle, a butcher from Newcastle, accompanied by his dog, set out on 26 March on business to Morpeth. He travelled without interruption until he arrived at Gosforth where four men approached him. The men were John Slater, James Henry, James Kelly and John Macbeth. The latter asked Buddle the time to which he replied it was not yet 1 am. Macbeth then asked for money to which Buddle replied that he only had four pence on his person. Macbeth became angry and, grasping his victim by the leg, threw him to the ground, put his hand over his mouth and held him while the other three men rifled his pockets of a little over £19. They did not get the money easily as both Buddle and his dog struggled and fought with them. Macbeth told the others to run, which they did with him hot on their heels. As the four robbers jumped over a gate and

Morpeth market place in the nineteenth century from a painting by Dugdale. William Buddle was travelling here when he was attacked. Author's collection

began to run across a field Buddle got up and pursued them. Buddle's dog managed to reach Macbeth and severely and repeatedly bite him on his heels. Macbeth kept running while shouting in pain. The men in front had pistols and were firing them at Buddle and his dog as they ran. They reached Seaton Burn and the first man managed jump over but the second and third men fell in before scrabbling to the other side. Macbeth went in head first and was plunged in mud. Buddle jumped in after him and began hitting Macbeth with a stick. The dog was also in the burn and bit every exposed part of Macbeth that he could. This conflict had been going on about ten minutes when Kelly mounted the dyke and pulling out a stake, hit Buddle over the temple and then the head with it. Buddle went under the water and then rose up again and continued the conflict beating Macbeth without mercy. Another of the gang beat Buddle with a stake until it broke. Macbeth was at the end of his tether and in a bid to escape his opponent threw himself onto the hedge at the side of the burn nearly impaling himself on a stake as he did so. Two of his accomplices carried Macbeth some distance away until he recovered himself. The man who had been holding the money had scarpered.

Buddle had been senseless for a time but when he came round, by now bleeding profusely, he went in pursuit of his

A map showing the location of Seaton Burn and the Six Mile Bridge. The Landmark Series: Ordnance Survey, Northumberland 1864

attackers. He came to a plantation at a Seaton Burn house where he was obliged to stop. The dog, however, stayed in pursuit for some distance. Buddle made his way to a public house at Six Mile Bridge arriving about 2 am. The family that ran the public house had retired to bed but arose to tend to Buddle's wounds. Later a party of butchers arrived and Buddle went out with them to try and track down the robbers but with no success. Buddle eventually returned home arriving at about 5.30 am.

Macbeth and Kelly were eventually captured at Durham and taken to Morpeth gaol. Slater and Henry managed to make it as far as Leicestershire before they were apprehended on 24 April and placed in a house of correction at Southwell in Nottinghamshire.

The culprits were charged with five robberies in Northumberland. On 2 August they were tried before Baron Bolland at Newcastle and sentenced to death. They could have quite easily murdered Buddle as at least two of the four men were armed. It was decided that they had not contemplated murder so their sentences were changed to transportation for life. Buddle, for his heroism, was given back the money he lost and was also presented with 'a splendid watch'.

CHAPTER 9

Murder and Arson at the Savings Bank 1838

Joseph Millie was from North Shields. On his father's death he had taken over the business as an ironmonger to support himself and his mother. The business eventually began to fail so Millie sold everything and paid off all his creditors. After this he tried to keep in employment of one sort or another to make a living. In about 1818 he was working for Wilson, a York hatter. In 1831 he was employed as a schoolmaster at the Ouseburn. Various other jobs took Millie to Newcastle, Gateshead and North Shields. In May of 1835, his wife died leaving him with five children. The youngest child died soon after. In 1836 he was working for a millwright in Chester-le-Street. Millie had, from time to time, been employed in the Newcastle Savings Bank on a temporary basis. On 5 December 1838, when he was fifty-six-years-old, he was given a permanent position as an assistant clerk within the bank.

Archibald Bolam was born on 9 August 1797 at Harbottle in Northumberland. He kept a school at Holystone and then in 1813 worked for George Gouin at his school in High Friar Street, Newcastle. Bolam then opened a school at Caistron, near Rothbury.

A sketch of Joseph Millie who was found brutally murdered at the Newcastle Savings Bank. Author's collection

In 1818 he was employed as an usher at Mr Bruce's school in Percy Street, Newcastle. Bolam worked in various other schools after that until he entered the Newcastle Savings Bank in about 1820.

Just before 2 am on 7 December, a fire was discovered in the waiting room of the Newcastle Savings Bank in the Arcade. Fire engines were called and the fire was extinguished fairly quickly. Doors, windows, window shutters and wainscoting had been damaged. A group of men entered the building to ascertain the extent of the damage. One of the men in the party came upon the body of a man lying face down on the hearth rug in front of the fire place. The lights were turned on and the body turned over. The men were sickened by the spectacle before them. The body was that of Joseph Millie, hardly recognizable because of the wounds to his face and head. His left jaw and cheek bone were broken, there were three large gashes to the left temple and his head was beaten almost to a pulp. There were about twenty wounds to the skull, all quite large. Blood and brains were spattered all over the hearth rug, wainscoting and walls. Beside

A sketch of Archibald Bolam who was found guilty of the murder of Joseph Millie and sentenced to transportation. Author's collection

the body was a pair of tongs and a poker. The poker was bent out of shape and was covered in blood and hair. Millie's pockets were stuffed with paper and coals and near to the body was a pile of papers. It was obvious that these had been meant to fuel the fire so as to destroy any evidence of murder. The men stood in shock for some length of time but eventually they began to look around the rest of the room. In the far corner was another man, seemingly unconscious. It was Archibald Bolam. Blood was seeping from a wound to the side of his neck. He was taken to a house in Pilgrim Street to have his wound attended to.

When Bolam regained consciousness he told his story to William Woods and Mr Alderman. He stated that he had received, at his home in Gateshead, two anonymous letters threatening him with harm. On Thursday evening another letter had arrived, this time, put under the door of the bank. Usually the bank was not left unattended but everyone had already left, including Millie, although he usually took his tea at the bank before he went home. Bolam was so upset by the letter he locked the door and he also went home to warn his housekeeper of the threat. He returned a little later finding the door locked as he had left it. On entering the bank, Bolam said he found Millie lying on the hearth rug. He assumed that Millie had let himself in with his own key and had fallen asleep in front of the fire. Bolam left Millie, intending to wake him later and walked towards his own desk. He stated that he then felt something strike him on the right temple. When Bolam turned around he saw a man in disguise and with a blackened face. He tried to call for help but the man threatened

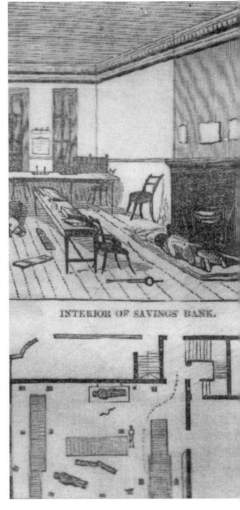

INTERIOR OF SAVINGS' BANK.

The murder scene and a ground plan of the Newcastle Savings Bank. The bank was a branch of the larger Bank of England in Grey Street. Author's collection

Bolam with death and then knocked him down and cut him in the neck. He passed out but vaguely remembered hearing a man walking about the room. The next time Bolam woke he could smell smoke but he then passed out again.

An examination of everyone involved was carried out in the long room at the *Blue Posts* in Pilgrim Street. Bolam, Millie's son, the people who discovered the fire and the body were questioned. Bolam was then taken into custody. Hand bills were posted with a reward of £100 for information leading to the discovery of the perpetrator.

On Wednesday, 12 December the inquest was resumed in the police office in the Manors. This time Mary Walker, Bolam's housekeeper, was questioned. Her statements were so contradictory that she was detained in custody to be examined privately by Alderman Batson. Mary Walker was eventually discharged. In about January of 1839 further rumours about the case had reached the ears of the authorities and Mary Walker was again examined. She was then detained in custody as an accessory after the fact. She was later released as no indictment was preferred against her.

The Royal Arcade where the Savings Bank was situated. Author's collection

On the morning of Monday, 4 March Bolam was taken from the gaol to the Guildhall to await the opening of the court. Throngs of people had assembled on the Sandhill long before the start of the trial. The public opinion against Bolam was strong. When the court doors were opened the room was full in no time. As the clock struck nine Baron Parke, his colleague Baron Alderson, the mayor and the sheriff entered the court. Bolam was brought in attended by officers of the police. Bolam's counsel asked that the removal of the trial to the county and it be postponed to the Summer Assizes to give a chance for public

The Bank of England in Grey Street, mother bank to the Newcastle Savings Bank. Author's collection

opinion to die down and to give a fairer trial. This was granted and Bolam was removed to the Moot Hall in the Castle Garth where he was arraigned. He pleaded not guilty and it was ordered that he be detained in the county gaol at Morpeth in the hope that if he were further away things would quiet down a little. On Sunday, 28 July Bolam was taken to the cells under the Moot Hall to await his trial the following morning. The conjecture that public opinion may have died a little was wrong. The Hall was densely packed with people awaiting the outcome of the trial. The case was heard before Baron Maule and the jury was made up of farmers, yeomen and gentlemen of Northumberland.

Entrance to the Side from Sandhill. Throngs of people had collected at the Sandhill to watch Bolam's trial. Author's collection

It was widely known that Bolam had always treated Millie with kindness and that the two were close friends. There seemed to be no motive for Bolam to have murdered Millie. In fact the porter of the bank said that when he left the premises

The railway arch at the foot of Dean Street where Bolam had been seen on the evening of Millie's murder. Author's collection

that afternoon Bolam and Millie were sitting together 'like brothers.'

A pane of glass had been heard to be broken in one of the bank's windows at about 5 pm that fateful day. On examination it was found it had been broken from the outside. When Bolam was arrested a key was found on his person which he said was to the front door of his house. On investigation it was discovered that the key belonged to his back yard. Neighbours had heard that door open and shut several times before 10 pm on the night of the fire. This suggested that Bolam had returned home more than once that evening. Bolam had been seen by two people proceeding in a hurried manner up the Side, past the foot of Dean Street and up to the higher part of the Side at a little before 7 pm. This was not his usual route to work. The pile of papers that had been near Millie's body had consisted of obsolete files and

The interior of the Warrior, *a convict ship used for transportation to Australia. Conditions aboard these ships would have been a punishment in itself.* Author's collection

other rubbish that had not been collected at random but carefully selected. This pointed to someone not wanting to destroy documents that might upset the running of the bank. When the premises were searched after the fire the water in the wash basin was found to be very dirty and one of the towels was bloodstained. There was no blood on the floor at the spot where Bolam was found although he had a neck wound. Mary Walker had stated at the first inquest she attended that she had assisted Bolam in cleaning the blood from his coat sleeves but her evidence was not brought up at the trial. Bolam's clothes were examined and what looked like blood and water was found on his shirt sleeves.

The judge summed up all the evidence in a long speech stating that it was circumstantial. He suggested that if the jury were to find Bolam guilty it should be of manslaughter and not murder. After retiring for three hours the jury brought in a verdict of manslaughter. The judge concluded by sentencing Bolam 'to be transported beyond the sea for the term of his natural life.' Bolam replied 'My Lord, I regard that sentence as my death.' He was then heard to say that he would rather have been hanged at once. Bolam left the dock amid hissing and clapping from the spectators.

Bolam was confined in Morpeth gaol until 31 August 1839, when he was placed upon the *Attwood* to be conveyed upon the hulks until his sailing for Botany Bay.

CHAPTER 10

They Were Only Prostitutes
1840–86

10.1 Sandgate, 1840:

Margaret Reay kept a house of ill repute in Cellar's entry in Sandgate. Four girls lived in the house including Martha Miller and Jane White, who was twenty. On Sunday, 15 March Martha brought James Moore home as a customer. The two were in Martha's room when they began to argue. Jane entered the room to see what the noise was about and Moore ordered her out. Jane began shouting at Moore so he picked up a lighted candle and set fire to the two shawls that Jane was wearing. By the time the flames were extinguished Jane was severely burnt on the breast, back and face. She was taken to the infirmary but died two days later.

Moore was tried at the Newcastle Summer Assizes and found guilty of manslaughter. He was sentenced to four months imprisonment.

Sandgate in the eighteenth century, where Margaret Reay kept her house of ill repute. Author's collection

10.2 The Quayside, 1869:

Matilda Martin, an Irishwoman who was thirty-nine, had been living with William Renwick as his wife for more than fifteen years. In August or September of 1869 Renwick left Matilda as they had had an argument. Matilda was given to heavy drinking and 'unchaste' habits.

George Weirs, who was originally from Middlesbrough, was a fireman on the steamer *Fusilier* which ran between Newcastle and Hull and was at this time docked at Newcastle. As was the usual when in port the crew would be looking for a good time. George and two of the other crewmembers went into the town to have a drink and a few laughs.

Matilda met up with a friend on the Quayside between 11 pm and 12 pm one Wednesday night. While they were walking between Spicer's Lane and Cox's Chare three young men

A 1914 sketch by Robert JS Bertram of Newcastle Quayside. Author's collection

THE QUAYSIDE.

approached, the crewmen from the *Fusilier,* and began to speak to the two women. The men offered to buy some drink. Matilda went into Mr Taylor's *Highlander Inn* in Pandon and bought 1/6p (7.5p) worth of whisky. They all went to Matilda's house to drink the whisky. They drank, sang, talked and apparently spent a pleasant hour or so. A couple of hours later, perhaps about 2 pm, Weirs left the house and Matilda followed him. The other two men and Matilda's friend stayed where they were. Fifteen minutes or so went by and then there was a loud cry from outside: 'Police I'm stabbed with a knife'. The three went out and at the top of the Burn Bank they found Matilda lying on her side on the ground. On turning her over they saw a wound on her chest that was bleeding profusely. The two young men went for the police.

When the police arrived and lifted Matilda's head she mumbled something. Nobody who heard her was sure whether she said 'a man' or 'my man'. Matilda died a short time later. In her pocket were a sovereign ($£1$) and a shilling (5p). There was also an apple with a sixpence (2.5p) pressed into it. When Weirs was brought into the police station to see Matilda he said 'that is the woman who robbed me.' He said she had robbed him of a pound in gold and three shillings in silver.

At the inquest held on Friday, 26 November witnesses were called to give statements. One was Mary Ellison, who lived in Pandon. She had heard a shout at about 2 pm on the night of the murder and had, after some delay because she was frightened, gone to her window. She heard a woman cry out that she had been stabbed. Mary then went to her door and described how she saw Weirs standing over Matilda. Other witnesses included Matilda's friend and the two young crewmen. A policeman also stated that he had passed Weirs just before Matilda was found. Weirs had told the policeman that he had been robbed by a prostitute.

Even though all the evidence pointed to Weirs being the perpetrator he was freed. The jury of twelve men brought in a verdict of 'murder, but by whom there was insufficient evidence to show.'

10.3 Dean Street, 1886

John Henry Fenning was a thirty-one-year-old blacksmith and fitter from Newcastle. He was married at St Andrew's Church on 7 January, 1886. After a few short months of marriage his wife left him and went back to live with her mother. She then took Fenning to court for maintenance, he was ordered to pay her 5s (25p) a week. Fenning became very angry and as he left the court he was uttering threats against his wife. A few days later he went on a drinking binge to the public houses near to

St Andrew's Church in 2003. It was here that Fenning was married in 1886.
The author

where his estranged wife and her mother lived. When Fenning was quite drunk he went and knocked on his mother-in-law's door but although he knocked continuously for a long period of time he was refused entrance. Later on that evening he left the area and went to the *Pink Lane* public house in Low Bridge where he picked up a prostitute, Annie Richardson, and they headed to her lodgings in Blyth Nook, Cowgate. They were in bed together when Annie's landlord, William Baker came in and told them to leave as he did not want such goings on at his premises. Fenning, before leaving, produced a cut-throat razor from his pocket and told Baker that he was going to use it on his wife. Late that night in Dean Street, Fenning was seen talking to another prostitute, Elizabeth Tait. She and Fenning headed to her lodgings at Peterson's in Low Bridge but when they arrived at the door they were refused entrance.

Shortly after midnight on 26 November Elizabeth Tait was found in a narrow lane off Dean Street. She was lying on the ground with her throat cut and a large gash to her forehead. Within a short space of time she had bled to death. A man dressed in black had been seen by several people at this time running towards Pilgrim Street. In fact, because he was running and must have looked suspicious, a policeman, Constable Weatherhead, who had been standing on the corner of Mosley Street, had stopped the man and asked his name which he gave as Daniel Feeney. He had also given a false address. When Elizabeth was found the police questioned some of the residents that lived nearby which led them to go to Fenning's house at 16 Prince's Street and arrest him. He had blood on his clothes and recent scratches on his hands but no weapon was found. A few of the neighbours had heard Elizabeth Tait in an altercation with a man as they left the lodgings at Low Bridge. The neighbours thought, that by the words that were spoken, Elizabeth had taken the man's wallet and he had discovered the theft.

Although the police and the prosecution were sure that Fenning was the murderer there was not enough evidence to convict him. They decided to enlist the help of two felons that were in Newcastle gaol at the same time Fenning was arrested.

One was Samuel Brindle who was on remand for stealing. Samuel stated that when he had asked Fenning why he was in custody, Fenning had replied that he had nearly cut a woman's head off and that he would have killed his wife too if he had had time. He also told Brindle that when he was running away a policeman had stopped him and he had given a false address. On Brindle asking if they had found the knife, Fenning had replied that it was not a knife that he had used but a chisel that he had sharpened.

The second felon was Thomas Trinity who was accused of stealing money from a ship at Berwick-on-Tweed. He stated that he had been in the reception room of the prison with Fenning and had asked him what he was in for. Fenning had replied that he had murdered a woman. Fenning had then gone on to tell Trinity that he had prepared a tool to kill his wife because she had taken out an order of maintenance against him.

Dean Street, where Elizabeth Tait was murdered. Author's collection

Fenning's workmates enlisted the services of a good defence. The defence argued that if Fenning was guilty, where was the weapon? It was brought to the attention of the court that the felon, Brindle, was an-ex policeman who had previously been incarcerated for false pretences so the chances of him telling the truth was in question. In fact the character of both felons that were called as witnesses were dubious whereas Fenning was of good character and had never been in trouble before. Fenning's wife also spoke up for him saying that he was a good and kind husband when not in drink.

Although blood was found on Fenning's clothes, he had been heard to make threats towards his wife and he was the last person to be seen with the murdered woman, the jury took just over half an hour to agree with the defence and John Fenning walked free from court.

In the present legal system, even though Jane White was a prostitute, the sentence on James Moore would surely have been more severe than just four months in prison.

Elizabeth Tait was described as being quiet and inoffensive although she had been locked up once or twice for being drunk. She also had two small children. The fact remained that both Elizabeth Tait and Matilda Martin were prostitutes and most likely thieves, therefore, they were the lowest form of scum on the social ladder. Their accused killer was tried by 'twelve good men and true' some of whom had probably lain with one of these two women or another 'Lady of the Night' at some time. Although it was not spoken about it was acceptable to use the services of a prostitute but their life and death meant nothing.

CHAPTER 11

The Stabbing of an Apprentice 1841

John Donkin was nineteen and lived with his father in the Back Lane at Gallowgate. Donkin was an apprentice to Henry Robson who was a shoemaker and had a shop at Eldon Lane, Percy Street. Three other men, Henry Stokoe, Thomas Heppel and William Cattermole were also employed in the shop. Cattermole was about thirty and was often made the butt of jokes by his workmates and customers as he was considered to be of weak intellect.

On Thursday, 15 April there were three customers in the shop, Robert Oxley, Fenwick Chambers and a man only known as Cruddace. During the morning, as a joke, a customer named Pattison had taken Cattermole's watch from where he normally hung it. Cattermole had become quite distressed when he discovered the watch missing. He was sent on an errand and the watch was put back in its place. Soon after another customer took Cattermole's cap from his head and, after immersing it in a pail of water, threw it back to him. He dried his cap by the fire and put it back on his head without seeming unduly upset. Just before noon Donkin snatched Cattermole's cap from his head again and threw it across the room. Cattermole raised a shoe he had in his hand but Donkin rose from his seat and warded off the ensuing blow. Cattermole then seized a knife that was lying on the seat where Donkin had left it. Before anyone saw what was coming Cattermole had stabbed Donkin in the thigh, calmly sat back down and resumed his work.

Seeing that blood was gushing from Donkin's wound and that he was quite faint, Hepple and Chambers assisted him to his chair while Stokoe went for medical help. On the arrival of Mr Turner, the surgeon, Donkin was given a small drink of spirit with water to revive him. Mr Turner applied a tourniquet to the main artery and dressed the wound. Donkin was put to bed in the house of his master until Saturday when it was considered safe to take him to his father's house. On Sunday the wound turned septic and on Monday morning the young man died.

A coroner's inquest was held on Monday before William Stoker and a jury of twelve men. Evidence was given by those that were present in the shop on the day of the stabbing and the jury found Cattermole guilty of manslaughter and committed him to be tried at the Newcastle Summer Assizes. At Cattermole's trial it was decided that if he had not been tormented as he was on that day he would never have hurt anyone. He received a sentence of one month's imprisonment.

CHAPTER 12

Domestic Violence, Drink and Death
1844–98

12.1 Blandford Street, 1844:

Mark Sherwood and his wife, Ann, lived in two cellar rooms under a house in Blandford Street, Newcastle. Sherwood was Irish and had been a soldier in the Artillery so received a small pension. The couple lived in abject poverty which was not helped by the fact that Sherwood spent what money he had on drink. The couple quarreled continuously with Ann using language that would have upset even the most placid of men, which Sherwood was not. On 13 March Ann and her husband argued throughout most of the day. The following morning no sound came from their apartment, and because this was so unusual, Ann's niece, Ann Sutherland, became suspicious. She borrowed a key from Walter Ormston, who lived in an adjoining house, and let herself in to the Sherwood's apartment; Her suspicions that all was not well were correct. There was blood everywhere and her aunt was lying on the floor with her head almost severed from the body. Lying beside Ann was her husband, whom at first the niece thought was also dead, but he was merely unconscious from the effects of drinking whisky. The niece alerted neighbours who in turn sent for the police. Inspector Little of Westgate police station arrived closely followed by two surgeons, Dr's Carr and Taylor. On examination of Ann's body it was found that she had two deep gashes on her throat, two horrific wounds on her lower jaw, cuts all over her hands and arms and one of her thumbs was nearly severed. The conclusion was that the cuts on Ann's hands and arms were caused as she tried to defend herself against her husband's attack but she did not stand a chance against his drunken, violent rage.

The doctors then turned their attention to Sherwood. He was still unconscious so a stomach pump was used to drain off the alcohol. Mustard blisters were applied to his hands and feet and within a short space of time the effects of the whisky had worn off. On looking through the apartment Inspector Little found a still where Sherwood had been making his own spirits. This home made whisky would have been far stronger than anything bought over the counter.

Sherwood stood trial at the Summer Assizes before Chief Baron Pollock who found him guilty of his wife's murder and sentenced him to death. Some of the influential people of the town had a petition drawn up to change Sherwood's sentence to transportation. The petition was unsuccessful and Sherwood was hanged on the Town Moor on 23 August by the executioner, Murdock of Glasgow. Sherwood was buried within the confines of the prison. His was the last execution to be carried out on the Town Moor.

12.2 The Side, 1850:

Patrick Forbes, a forty-year-old Irish labourer, lived with his wife, Elizabeth, their son, Thomas and their daughter Bridget in Clogger's Entry at the head of the Side in Newcastle. On 29 March the couple spent the full day drinking in *Robertson's* spirit shop. Elizabeth was so drunk she could hardly walk. Two neighbours, Elizabeth Dees and Mrs Wheatley, helped her up the stairs. Forbes and his wife then went to bed. Thomas was asleep in the same room. Through the night Bridget entered the room several time to get bread. When she went in Bridget had heard snoring but she did not know who it was.

The following morning when Bridget returned to the room her mother was laying half out of the bed. The quilt was soaked with blood. Bridget ran for help and a policeman who was near by heard her cries of 'murder' and returned to the room with her. It was stated that there were no visible injuries on the body at that time but later wounds that may have been inflicted with a knife were found. Knives were found in Forbes' pockets and he was arrested for the murder.

On 31 July Justice Wightman sentenced Forbes to death. On 23 August, the day prior to his execution, he made an

Looking through the railway arch to the Side. The Forbes family lived here in Clogger's Entry. Author's collection

official statement declaring that he loved his wife dearly and could not remember attacking her. Forbes also said that he was very drunk and he had no thought or intention of hurting his wife. He felt that he had a fair trial and as there was no other person that could have committed the deed that night he knew it was he and he surrendered himself to the laws of the country.

The Side opposite the Butcher's Bank. Author's collection

Executions were usually held on the Town Moor but this time the scaffold was erected in Carliol Square. The landlord of the *Newcastle Arms,* the only public house in the vicinity, took payment for window seats. Bets were laid as to how many people would attend the spectacle and the whole atmosphere was one of a public holiday. By the time the execution was to take place a huge crowd had turned out to watch. Forbes had to be assisted to walk to the scaffold. He was pale and trembling and those nearest to him could hear him praying. The executioner was seventy-four-year-old Howard of York who was commonly known as Jack Ketch. He was jeered and hissed at by the crowd. When the bolt was withdrawn Forbes did not fall correctly but was half on and half under the scaffold. The executioner hastily pulled him up and let him drop again and after a minute or so Forbes was dead. He was buried within the confines of the prison near to the body of Mark Sherwood.

A map showing Carliol Square where a gallows was erected for the hanging of Patrick Forbes. Ordnance Survey, Central Newcastle 1914

12.3 South Shields 1869:

John Tracey, who was thirty-eight, his wife Jane and their three children aged eight weeks, three years and five years all lived in a cellar kitchen at the back of East Adelaide Street in South Shields. Margaret Dykes, whose husband, John, was a seaman, lived above the cellar and the two families used a shared access to their rooms.

On the evening of 14 March Margaret Dykes had gone downstairs and saw Jane cooking her husband's supper. Jane was not quite sober but still capable of doing her chores. Later that night at about 10 o'clock Margaret was near her window when she heard Jane say 'Come away Christy, we'll get some beer'. She was speaking to a man named Christopher

Market Place, South Shields.

The Market Place in South Shields around 1863. Author's collection

Donahoe. Margaret then saw Jane and Donahoe walk up the back lane. She heard them return at about 11.45 and Tracey asking Jane where she had been. Then Jane began to scream and Margaret heard Tracey shout 'I'll kill you for spending my money.' Other neighbours that lived in the house had heard the commotion and came out of their rooms and downstairs to see what was going on. By this time Jane had run into the wash house which was below the cellar. Her husband had heavy work clogs on his feet and he was kicking her with all his force. Someone pulled him away and the police were sent for. Sergeant Thomas Ayrey of the South Shields police force was quickly at the scene. He found Jane Tracey, in obvious pain, lying at the foot of the cellar stairs with blood from the lower part of her body forming a pool around her. Within minutes she was dead. Ayrey entered the kitchen to find Tracey and Donahoe sitting by the fire both very drunk. Tracey's clogs were covered in blood. He was arrested and charged with the murder of his wife.

The medical examination showed that Jane had suffered severe injuries to the lower part of her body. The amount of blood she had lost was sufficient in itself to have caused death.

At the trial, Christopher Donahoe said that he and Tracey were labourers at the Tyne Chemical Works. They had left work between one and two o'clock on the afternoon of 14 March and had gone to a beer-house to divide their wages. They had gone back to the Tracey's room at about six that evening. Donahoe had then fallen asleep. He said he did not remember going with Jane for more beer that night.

When Tracey gave his evidence he at first said that he had heard Jane fall in the wash-house but later admitted that he was drunk and had 'Given it to her.' He stated that Donahoe and Jane had gone for another gallon of beer that night and he was jealous because he had heard them laughing together.

Tracey was found guilty only of manslaughter, possibly the jury thought that because Jane had been drinking she had partly brought it on herself. The judge did, however, make a statement saying that Tracey had given way to brutal passions which deserved the severest form of punishment and sentenced Tracey to fifteen years in penal servitude.

12.4 Mitford Street, 1874:

John William Anderson was a thirty-two-years-old clerk. He had previously been a private in the 98th Regiment and a clerk in the 28th Regiment and was well respected. He lived with his wife, Elizabeth and a son at Mitford Street in Newcastle. Their elder son, who was nine, lived with Anderson's mother.

On the evening of 28 August the couple had been for a drink and neither was sober when they returned home. Later witness statements reported that the pair had been on good terms before leaving the beer shop but were heard to quarrel on returning to the house. Their young son came home at about ten that night and Anderson was apparently not going to allow him to enter the house. Elizabeth was heard to say to her husband 'you won't lock the boy out.' Anderson had then gone to the door and approached their son. The boy had backed away and began to cry so Anderson shut the door. Elizabeth had then argued with her husband saying she would let the

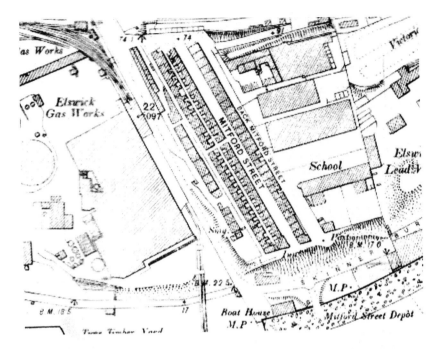

Map showing Mitford Street where John Anderson murdered his wife. Ordnance
Survey, Newcastle & Gateshead 1894

boy in herself but by this time the boy had run away. Because
Anderson had refused to let her open the door Elizabeth
struck him. Anderson started to call his wife names and a
scuffle had then taken place. Anderson was heard to threaten
to stab his wife if she hit him again. Two screams were then
heard, the second dying off into a moan. Kit Danskin's kitchen
backed on to the Anderson house separated only by a door.
She had heard the altercation and when everything went quiet
Kit went into the house to check that Elizabeth was okay. She
found her neighbour lying behind a counter barely breathing.
Sarah Dodds and George Dodds lived in Tyneside Terrace and
they also had heard the commotion. They ran over to the
Mitford Street house and as they did so Anderson was coming
through the front door. As he passed them he said 'I've
finished her'. A little later Anderson walked into the police
station. His hand was bleeding and he told the police that
Elizabeth had stabbed him first so he had stabbed and killed

William Marwood, executioner 1874-83. Brian Elliott collection

her. On a medical examination it was found that Elizabeth had been stabbed three times. One wound was above the left hip, one in the back and one through the heart.

At the trial held at the Newcastle Winter Assizes before Justice Denman, neighbours said that the couple had been on good terms until about two years previously when Elizabeth, although not a habitual drunkard, began drinking frequently. Elizabeth's father contradicted this statement saying that his daughter was a sober person and a good wife and mother.

After a short deliberation the jury found Anderson guilty of murder but with a strong recommendation to mercy. Anderson stated in court that he did not deserve clemency and deserved to die for what he had done. Numerous petitions were sent in his favour but the Home Secretary declined to interfere. He was hanged on 23 December 1875 by William Marwood. His was the first private execution to be held at Newcastle and took place within the gaol.

12.5 Pine Street, 1890:

Lily McLarence Wilson married John Myers, a water cart driver in Manchester, to whom she had two children, both boys. Lilly then met William Row, a shoemaker, for whom she left her husband. Taking the two children, Lily and Row moved to 4 Pine Street, Newcastle. On the late afternoon of 3 January Lily was found dead with her throat cut.

The chief witness to what had taken place that fateful day was Lily's eight year-old son, John. At the inquest he told the court that he had left his mother and Row sitting talking. He had gone into the next room to play with the landlady's son. About ten minutes went by when he heard his mother scream.

John returned to the room and saw his mother seated on a chair and Row standing behind her with a knife in his hand. Row then pulled Lily onto the floor, bent over her and cut her throat. Helen Tait, the landlady, had heard the screams and come into the room from next door. Meanwhile Row calmly put on his hat and jacket and left the house. John also told the court that on Christmas Eve there had been two young men in the house laughing and singing with Lily. Row had ordered them out and then he and Lily had words about the matter.

Mrs Tait stated that she kept a lodging house and Row and Lily had moved in about the middle of October 1889. They had told her they had been married about a year and previous to that Lily had been a widow and Row a widower. Mrs Tait said that there had been no trouble until Christmas Eve when she had heard the couple quarrelling. Row had been drinking but did not seem drunk.

On the day in question, Mrs Tait stated that Lily had come into her room and put a kettle on the stove and then returned to her own room. Minutes later there was a scream then the sound of dishes breaking. There was a second scream so Mrs Tait had gone to investigate. She saw Row bending over Lily who was lying in front of the fire. Lily's son was standing in the room shouting 'Mama.' Mrs Tait went to pull Row away from Lily when the boy shouted to her that Row was cutting his mother's throat. She then saw the knife in Row's hand and realized that Lily was bleeding profusely.

PC Rose was on the beat outside when he heard children crying. John Myres then ran up to him and said his mother was dead. The policeman followed the boy into the house and found Lily's body. There was blood all over the room and a shoemaker's knife lying beside the body. Dr Cross was called and he found six knife wounds around the neck and face. Two to the neck were deep and long and, in his opinion, either could have caused death.

At the Assizes it transpired that Row thought Lily was being unfaithful to him and the anger had been building up in him since Christmas Eve. He had taken the knife into the house with the sole intention of doing her harm. It took the jury two hours and thirty-five minutes to find Row guilty but with a strong recommendation to mercy. His Lordship pointed out that there was nothing to show Lily had been unfaithful to Row but that he had induced her to be unfaithful to her husband. He also said that there had been nothing to justify this brutal murder and he was therefore sentencing Row to death.

William Row was hanged at Newcastle on 12 March 1890 by James Berry.

12.6 Gateshead, 1897:
Thirty-three-year-old Charles Smith and his wife, Mary Ann, who was twenty-seven, had married when Mary Ann was about eighteen. The couple had come from Aberdeen with their two

James Berry, executioner, 1884-92.
Author's collection

children about nine months previously. An adopted nephew, who was about five, also lived with them. They occupied one room upstairs in a house at 22 Pipwellgate in Gateshead. Their room was reached by eight stone steps from outside. Next door to them lived a Mrs Connolly. The two houses were separated by a passage that ran down to the river. Most of the nearby buildings were warehouses so the two occupied houses were fairly isolated. Smith, who was a plasterer, had worked for the same firm for ten years in his hometown of Aberdeen before moving to Gateshead. He, along with other men, was employed working on some houses at Jesmond.

On Monday, 27 December Smith left his work at noon in the company of a co-worker. The pair visited various public houses in Newcastle having a few glasses in each. They eventually went to Smith's house in Pipwellgate where Mary Ann was sitting by the fire partially dressed. She told her husband she had just got out of bed. The two men and Mary Ann had some beer and then Smith changed out of his work-clothes. He lifted his accordion and the two men went back out. When Smith returned at about 9 o'clock that night some

The port of Gateshead around 1863. Author's collection

friends of theirs, Mr and Mrs MacDonald, came to the house. They left at about 11 pm to go home. The McDonalds' said afterwards that Smith and his wife were fine and were chatting amicably.

A little later that night, Smith went to the MacDonald's house and told them he had found Mary Ann in the water closet and that she had been murdered. The couple went with Smith back to his house and found his wife's body lying on the bed. Both of Mary Ann's eyes were black and swollen, her right eye was cut and blood was oozing from her nose. Her lips were bruised and it was obvious by other indications of violence that she had suffered some terrible injuries. There was blood on the side of the fire-place, on the wallpaper, on the pictures and even on the ceiling. There was also blood on the looking glass. The body of the woman had been washed and this accounted for water that mingled with blood on the floor. Smith was in his shirt-sleeves. There was blood on his shirt, vest and trousers and also on his face. On the floor were pieces of a broken broom handle. The pieces were smeared with blood and hair. A block of wood that was in the room was also covered in blood and hair.

A water closet of the nineteenth century. Cleveland County Council Libraries and Leisure Department

On the arrival of the police the water closet was inspected. The Smith's had exclusive use of this commodity and had a key. Inside was found Mary Ann's skirt and jacket and there was blood on the floor. The assumption was that the woman's clothes had been removed so as to wash the blood from her body. Smith denied having anything to do with his wife's death and demanded an investigation into who had killed her. The police did not believe Smith so he was arrested and charged with Mary Ann's murder. He later said that if he had killed his wife he could remember nothing about it.

On medical examination it was found, besides the injuries already mentioned, Mary Ann's body was covered in bruises. There were also two severe wounds to the head, one about six inches (50cm) the other about three inches (25cm) in length. Both wounds had exposed the bone of the skull.

The Smith's two children were questioned. Their son, who was eleven, remembered his father coming back to the house and after changing his clothes, going back out. The boy said his brother went to bed about 7 pm and his cousin about 9 pm. Smith came in and Mr MacDonald went and bought some beer. The men drank the beer and Mary Ann had a whisky. When the boy went to bed at about 11pm that night he remembered seeing the long handled broom under the table, intact at that time. The block of wood was one his father had brought in to burn on the fire. Later that night the boy was awoken by his younger brother who said that their mother was downstairs. The boy went downstairs and out to the water-closet where he saw his mother lying on the floor. He noticed that her eye was cut. She muttered something about going upstairs. Smith took hold of Mary Ann's head and body and her son took hold of her legs. They carried her upstairs and laid her on the floor. She only had a petticoat on and nothing else. The boy said his mother's eye was bleeding and her back was covered in dirt as if she had been dragged along the ground. Smith wiped Mary Ann's chest with a cloth and some water and they then lifted her onto the bed. She had not spoken again.

The son then told how his mother had pawned some of his father's clothes and they had had words about it earlier that week. It was brought up again that evening and Mary Ann had

The groined archway at Newgate in 1817 showing the preparation for the execution of Charles Smith. Author's collection

thrown a bottle at her husband's head before Mr and Mrs MacDonald had arrived. The blood that was on the looking glass was his father's from where the bottle glanced off the side of his head.

At his trial on 3 March 1898, the jury found Charles Smith guilty of beating the life out of Mary Ann with the broom and the block of wood that were to hand. The jury, because of the evidence given by the Smith's son of the circumstances, gave a strong recommendation for mercy but Justice Lawrence pronounced sentence of death.

A petition for a reprieve was prepared in Aberdeen of which a copy was published in the *Aberdeen Journal*. The petition stated that Charles Smith had been of good character according to both his employers and his workmates whilst he had lived and worked in Aberdeen. The petition was signed by magistrates and other leading citizens of the town. It was forwarded to the Home Secretary but the reprieve was denied and Charles Smith, still pleading his innocence, was hanged by William Billington on 22 March 1898.

12.7 Pilgrim Street, 1898:

Annie Hand and Daniel Fagan lived in a room at Church Walk, Pilgrim Street in Newcastle with their two children, Daniel who was about seven and Elizabeth who was nine. The couple, who were both in their mid forties, had lived together for many years. They had a tempestuous relationship and the other residents of the house were used to hearing them quarrel.

PC Alex Grey was on duty in Pilgrim Street on the evening of Saturday, 26 March. He was alerted to the fact that all was not well at 8 Church Walk. On going to investigate, he found Annie Hand lying at the top of the stairs quite obviously lifeless. Dr Baumgartner was called and he had Annie's body moved to the St Lawrence Mortuary. Until further investigations could be carried out, PC Grey took Fagan into custody. Fagan denied anything to do with Annie's death. He told PC Grey that he had not left the house since four that afternoon and that Annie had come in drunk and laid at the top of the stairs. PC Grey made a cursory examination of the

Pilgrim Street Gate in 1800. Author's collection

clothes Fagan was wearing and found nothing. He then searched Fagan's room and found a jacket with what looked like blood spots near the pockets. He also found a pair of boots that looked as though they had been washed but red spots were still visible. The room was in disarray, a table was on a lean with its leg broken and there was water all over the floor.

The trial was held at the Newcastle Police Court where there was no shortage of witnesses. Dr Baumgartner said that Annie was dressed in a black bodice, skirt and underskirt with no underwear. The clothing she had on was badly torn and saturated with blood. He had found superficial bruising all over Annie's body but the actual cause of death was loss of blood from a large deep wound on the lower part of her body. Death had taken place on the landing and as there was no weapon that could have been used the doctor concluded that the wound had been caused by a violent kick. Dr Baumgartner had also examined Fagan's clothes. He found no blood on the jacket but there were blood stains on the lower part of the trousers and on the boots. The doctor stated that he could not be certain that it was human blood.

Newcastle County Court in use from 1864-1993. Author's collection

The other residents of the house were called one by one. Mary Ann McGarry, Elizabeth Carlisle and her daughter, Martha, Mary Ann Picketts and Mary Ann Pickard all told the same story. They said that the couple were heavy drinkers, Annie perhaps more so than her partner. Annie had been drunk on Friday night but was sober on the Saturday afternoon. Although arguments often took place no one had ever seen Fagan lift his hands to Annie. On the evening in question the witnesses had heard the couple shouting at each other then the sound of splashing as if water was being thrown. There was the sound of a crash as if something or someone had fallen and then the door to their room banged shut. Annie was then on the landing and heard to say 'You murderer, you have finished me now.' Fagan then left the house. Not one of the witnesses went to check on Annie. A little while later Fagan returned and Mary Ann Picketts, who lived in the next room on the same landing, came to her door and saw Annie lying on the stairs with Fagan and his young son looking at her by candlelight. Mary Ann then went for a policeman.

Young Daniel was then brought in as a witness but he cried so much the coroner excused him. The daughter, Elizabeth, then told her story. She stated that her father was in the house when her mother came home with drink in her. They began to argue and her father threw a pail of water over her mother. He then kicked her twice and she fell. Fagan then dragged Annie to the stairs and left her there. He came back into the room and changed his boots washing the ones he had used to kick Annie. He then washed his hands, put on his coat and went out. Elizabeth went to bed leaving her mother lying on the stairs.

Because of Annie's dissolute habits the jury waived a murder verdict and found Fagan guilty only of manslaughter.

CHAPTER 13

Honour Thy Father and Mother
1845

Robert Joicey was fifty-seven and had two sons. One son, Ralph, lived with him, his wife and daughter at Cockle Park near Morpeth. The other son, William, lived at Hutton's Court, Pilgrim Street. Joicey had a minor ailment and was under the medical supervision of Dr Hedley of Morpeth who would frequently leave medicine for him at the *Portland Arms* public house for collection by the family.

On 9 December 1845 Robert Joicey died in his home. His appearance suggested he had died in agony under suspicious circumstances. On a post-mortem being carried out it was found his death had been caused by arsenic poisoning. The police were called in and they arrested Mrs Joicey, her daughter and then went in search of Ralph whom they found at his brother's house.

At the initial inquest there was no shortage of witnesses. Ann Richardson had lived in as a servant to the Joicey's for about six months until Martinmas. About two months before she left there was a quarrel within the family. Ann said that Robert began the argument and spoke 'very harshly'. His daughter had replied by telling him to beware or she would poison him. When the daughter was questioned she denied threatening to poison her father but he had called her all sorts of bad names. What she had said was that her father would put it into her head to play *The Lass of Acklington*; this was someone who had been accused of poisoning her father but had been acquitted. Dr Hedley gave evidence to the fact that on a previous occasion he had been called to attend Mrs Joicey. While he had been bleeding her she had shook her fist at her husband in anger but he did not know what the basis of that had been. Dr Hedley stated that the week before the death he had left two powders at the *Portland Arms* for Robert Joicey. One of the jurors was a neighbour of the family and knew them well. He stated that he had been in their house one night recently and had left because of the arguments. He added that, at the time, he was worried they would do each other harm. Mrs Joicey stated that she had collected three packages of powder from the public house and had given one to her husband that evening. He became very ill almost immediately. She did not call a doctor because she was afraid that there had been some 'mischief.' Her husband lingered for five days in extreme pain and then died. The police had established that about two months previously Ralph had purchased a quantity of arsenic from Mr Creighton, a chemist, in Morpeth. Mrs Joicey and her daughter were released and Ralph was charged with murder.

Ralph Joicey admitted to causing his father's death. He had mixed a considerable portion of the arsenic in two lots of jalap (a form of laxative) and, after disguising himself, had left the package at the public house. On the package was written 'I make you a present for Joicey. Take this large powder in a glass of ale or a glass of wine and the smaller one in a little honey or jelly, the one at night, the other in the morning.' This package, along with the two that Dr Hedley had left, was collected by Mrs Joicey. When asked why he had kept the arsenic so long before making sure it was administered to his father, Ralph said it was because when he bought it he was not sure whether he was going to use it or not. The reason he gave for the murder was because of the terrible way his father treated the family. When asked why he did not move away, Ralph said it was because he was frightened to leave his mother and sister by themselves with his father.

Ralph Joicey was tried at the Assizes before Justice Coleridge on 26 February 1846. After being found guilty of the murder of his father, Ralph was executed at a public hanging at Morpeth on 18 March the same year. His body was interred within the confines of the gaol. Joicey's execution was the first at Morpeth since 1822 and the event attracted huge crowds.

CHAPTER 14

The Irish Workers
1846–90

14.1 The Stabbing in a Field, 1846:

During the building of the Newcastle and Berwick railway both English and Irish workers were employed in its construction. On Monday, 5 October, during working hours, an argument had broken out between John Hughes and George Matthews, who were Irish and Daniel Hives, a carter, who was English. The cause of the altercation never came to light but later in the day Hughes and Matthews attacked Hives and then ran off. Hives was quite badly injured around the face and head but gave chase to his attackers.

Mrs Bryson, who lived at Willington George Pit at Long Benton was returning from Newcastle on the Monday afternoon when she saw two men running along the coach lane towards her, one of them carrying a stick. She then saw another man, his face all bloody, following the first two. As the third man approached Mrs Bryson asked him what was going on. He said that the two men he was chasing had used him badly and the Irish would not get the better of an Englishman. He added that he would run until he dropped to catch them. Mrs Bryson ran to a farm that adjoined Benton Lane to get help. The farm belonged to a magistrate, Captain Potts. Potts was standing at a stile at the bottom of Benton Lane. He had already spotted the men and heard one of them say 'You, I'll finish you, you go too far.' And then 'I'll murder you if you come any closer'. Their pursuer answered that he would follow as long as he had a drop of blood in him. Mrs Bryson and Potts saw the two men climb the stile into Dog Kennel Field with the third man close behind, so Potts followed. Unexpectedly, the two men being chased stopped and turned around allowing their pursuers to catch up with them. Potts stood between the men asking what the affray was over and trying to calm them down. He was pushed out of the way and there was a short scuffle. Hives fell to the ground and the other two took to their heels. Captain Potts shouted at the two to stop but they were already running, one in the direction of Byker Hill and the other over the fields. Potts went to the assistance of the injured man who was now back on his feet but there was blood pouring down and out of his trouser leg. Within minutes he fell to the ground, this time not to rise again. He had been fatally stabbed between the thigh and the abdomen. Potts went back to the lane and stopped a man on horseback telling him what had taken place and asking him to give chase to the two culprits. A butcher, William Blekinsopp, who was passing, also gave chase on foot.

The two men were later caught and the initial trial was held at Mr Boggin's *Black Bull* in Long Benton. They were then tried at the Moot Hall before Baron Rolfe on 27 February, 1847. Mrs Bryson and Captain Potts were able to identify Hughes and Matthews as the two men that Hives was chasing. Hughes was acquitted but Matthews was sentenced to death for the murder of Daniel Hives. He was executed at Morpeth on 17 March, 1847.

14.2 A Mysterious Death, 1890:
On 10 February 1890 Michael Conner was admitted to the Jarrow Memorial Hospital. He was very weak and in extreme pain and died within a short space of time. On a medical examination by Dr Smellie, Conner was found to have superficial bruises on the left cheek and temple. A small cut under the left eye. Under the left groin, over a large rupture that had occurred some years previously, there was the mark of a severe blow that had been recently inflicted with a blunt instrument. There was also a slight rupture to the right side of the groin. On the left knee and above the right ankle there was severe bruising also caused by a blunt instrument. Death was caused by an injury to the bowels.

At the inquest held at the Council Chambers in Jarrow presided over by coroner John Graham, the evidence was very conflicting. John Conner stated that on Saturday, 8 February he and his brother Michael had gone to the *Alkali Inn* at East Jarrow for a night out. They joined the company of another two men, James Patterson and Edward McCormick. The evening was going well with a bit of a sing-song and the drink flowing fast and furious. Patterson and Michael Conner both stated that they could sing as well as anyone in the room. A gallon of beer was offered to the best singer. Both men sang their individual songs and the majority of votes went to Patterson. The two men then began arguing as to who had the better voice. The argument turned nasty and Patterson punched Conner in the eye. Conner shoved Patterson who retaliated by punching him again, this time knocking him to the floor. Patterson then proceeded to kick the fallen man. (Most of the men present had their working clogs on). John Conner grabbed Patterson by a handkerchief that was around his neck and pulled him away from his brother. He then picked his brother up and sat him on a chair. McCormick then also punched the victim in the face so John Conner scuffled with McCormick. By this time someone had gone for the Conner's sister and she and John Conner took Michael home. His condition became worse so they took him to the Memorial Hospital about 10 pm on Monday where he died soon after.

Elizabeth Wears was a servant to John Bramwell, the landlord of the *Alkali Inn*, followed with her statement. She said that when the company voted Patterson the better singer both John and Michael began to argue with him. John struck Patterson who returned the punch shouting to stop as he did not want the two of them at him. Michael then punched Patterson who retaliated by knocking Michael to the ground. John then interfered again until he too fell to the floor. Their sister then came in and the three of them left with Michael being supported by her and John. Elizabeth stated that she had seen no one kicking anyone.

The coroner commented that the evidence was unsatisfactory and contradictory. John Conner's statements were not backed up by any other witnesses and it seemed to him that McCormick had not been involved at all.

The jury returned a verdict that Michael Conner had died in consequence of an injury to the bowel, but by whom and how caused there was insufficient evidence to show. McCormick and Patterson were dismissed.

It would seem in this case very little notice was taken of the medical evidence. According to Elizabeth there were only a few punches inflicted and all of these were to the face. How then did Michael have bruising to his legs and injuries to his groin?

CHAPTER 15

Murder at Matfen
1855

The serene and beautiful village of Matfen was the ancestral home of the Blackett family. Edward Blackett paid for the church of Holy Trinity in 1842 and Matfen became a separate parish in 1846. In 1855 the peacefulness of the little village was shattered by news of a brutal murder.

A short distance from the centre of the village, at a place named Waterloo there was a row of five cottages which were owned by Dorothy Bewicke, a lady of sixty-six years. The little houses were in a deplorable state. Rain leaked in, hens roosted in the roof and panes of glass were missing and had been replaced with any old rubbish that would cover the holes. Dorothy resided in one of the cottages, and, like many an eccentric, had gained the reputation of being wealthy.

On the morning of 21 October some of Dorothy's neighbours became worried when there was no sign of her out and about. They went to her cottage and on entering were shocked at what they found. Dorothy's body was lying upstairs on the bedroom floor. Her hands were tied across her breast with a leather strap and her legs tied together with a halter. It was obvious by the distinct finger marks on her throat that she had been strangled. Dorothy's little house had been thoroughly ransacked. Even the mattress of her bed had been cut open. Sacking had been put up against the front windows so anyone passing would not have seen the lights of the robbers as they searched her possessions.

One of Dorothy's cottages had been rented to a group of besom makers (this involved making brooms from twigs and was often done by gypsies) and suspicion fell on them. The group consisted of James Conroy, John Simm, Isabella Allan and her three children Michael, Jane and Ellen. All six were arrested and stood trial for murder before Justice Willes at Northumberland Assizes on 29 February 1856. Although there was circumstantial evidence and Simms turned witness for the Crown there was not enough to convict any of the suspects. After a trial lasting two days the prisoners were acquitted.

CHAPTER 16

All Because of a Dog Tax
1861

Most foul deeds are carried out behind closed doors or under a blanket of darkness. One exception to the rule took place on a cold winter's day in the town of Newcastle in 1861. It was about 9.30 on the morning of Tuesday, 1 October and the townsfolk had begun to go about their daily business.

Mark Frater, a Tax Collector, was walking to his office when he met a friend, Thomas Horn, in Northumberland Street. They walked to Frater's office, which was opposite Grey's Monument in Blackett Street, and stood talking at the door with their backs to the street. Suddenly, seemingly from nowhere, a man came up from behind and grabbed Frater. Frater tried to struggle free but the man, who was later identified as George Clark, held him in a tight grasp around the neck with one arm. The man then raised his other arm and

The east end of Blackett Street in 1840. Author's collection

BLACKETT·STREET

A 1914 sketch by Robert JS Bertram of Blackett Street where Mark Frater's office was situated. Author's collection

thrust downwards. As the attacker let go of his victim Frater put his hand to his cheek and Horn saw blood on his friend's cheek and neck. John Dalrymple was passing by when he saw two men struggling together. As he came towards them Dalrymple saw blood on the cheek of one of the men and a knife in the hand of the other. He grabbed hold of the attacker and wrested the knife from his grasp. Just at that moment Dr Septimus William Rayne happened to be passing in his

Grey Street and the Monument in the nineteenth century. The Monument was erected in 1938 to commemorate the services of Prime Minister, Charles, Earl Grey (1764-1845). Author's collection

carriage. On seeing that there was some sort of trouble he stopped to render assistance. Frater was, by this time, sitting on the step still holding his hand to a wound in his cheek. Dr Rayne helped the injured man upstairs to his office and sat him in a chair. When the doctor removed Frater's hand from the wound blood gushed out. The doctor put his fingers inside the wound to try and nip the blood vessels together but he realized that Frater's arteries were cut and his wind pipe was totally severed. Dr Rayne sent one of the office clerks to bring Dr Liddle and Dr Lightfoot to assist him. They arrived at the scene very quickly but although the three medical men did what they could Frater choked to death on his own blood within a short space of time.

Meanwhile, out in the street, Richard Wilson, who had a butcher's shop directly across from the Tax Office, Horn, Dalrymple and another passer-by, Mr McGilcray, took hold of Clark and escorted him to Prudhoe Street police station.

Clark was given into the custody of Police Constable George Anderson along with the knife Dalrymple had taken from Clark. On a search of the prisoner P C Anderson found an old receipt for two quarter's payment of dog tax and a notice from Frater stating that he had seized goods from Clark for non payment of dog tax. When he was charged with stabbing Frater, Clark said 'Decidedly so, decidedly so, I've murdered him, he robbed me and now I have robbed him'.

Clark's initial trial was held at the Manor's Police Court. When he was first arrested there was shock at the callousness of his behavior but his sanity was not questioned. As the trial went on serious doubts began to be raised as to his state of mind. Throughout his trial he interrupted, and at times, babbled almost incoherently. Witnesses came forward to state that Clark had a history of saying that he was suffering from wrongs inflicted upon him and would vow revenge against the people that were persecuting him. He had been heard on a few

A 1914 sketch by Robert JS Bertram of Grey's Monument. Author's collection

Manor's police station in 1845. It was here that George Clark's initial trial was held. Author's collection

occasions over the previous weeks to threaten Frater's life but the people he had spoken to did not know who Frater was or what he had done to upset Clark.

A month or so before the murder Frater had sent two of his clerks to seize goods from Clark for non payment of dog tax. Clark was a chair-maker and the goods seized were saws and other joinery tools. These tools were still in Frater's office. Clark told a witness that he had been in touch with the House of Lords and the Queen (Victoria) over this injustice. He then said that the Queen had told him that it would be okay for him to murder Frater for what he had done.

On examination of the knife that had been used in the stabbing it was found that the end of the blade had been cut to make it jagged. The post mortem on Frater showed that the knife had gone in through his cheek and then the jagged blade had been thrust and turned in the wound with such force that

Grey's Monument in 2003, now a central meeting place for shoppers and students.

it had penetrated down to the throat and severed several arteries.

At his final trial at the Assizes Clark was found guilty of the cold blooded murder of Mark Frater and sentenced to death. He was reprieved because of insanity and sentenced to be detained in a lunatic asylum for the rest of his life.

Was George Clark insane at the time of the attack or did he become unbalanced when he realized what he had done? The motive for the murder seems ridiculous but the seizure of his tools may not have been a trivial matter to Clark. These would have been the tools of his trade and perhaps without them he could not earn a proper living. On the other hand perhaps Clark was perfectly sane during and after the attack. He may have been a violent murderer and also a clever man who feigned his insanity so he would not have to face the rope.

CHAPTER 17

Rape and Murder at the West Walls 1863

argaret Docherty, previously Margaret Kennedy, married John, a tailor, in the Roman Catholic Church in Glasgow in 1832. They later moved to Buckingham Street in Newcastle. On New Years Day Margaret, by then about fifty years of age, and her husband had been drinking all evening. They finished up at *Ireland's* public house in Gallowgate. Docherty had asked his wife to come home but she refused. He pulled her outside and as he did so there were three men whom he did not recognize. One of the men hit Docherty and knocked him to the ground. Margaret was standing nearby as her husband got to his feet and went home.

A map showing the location of Buckingham Street where Margaret Docherty lived. Ordnance survey, Central Newcastle, 1914

The West Walls in the eighteenth century where the rape and murder of Margaret Docherty took place. Author's collection

He later said that he thought his wife would follow him. The next time Docherty saw Margaret was the following morning in the dead house. He was shown a cap, a pair of shoes and an apron that was saturated with blood which he said was what his wife had been wearing when he last saw her alive.

Two men had gone to the Westgate police station to report finding a woman's body near the West Walls. When the police followed them to the place indicated they were horrified at what they saw. Margaret's cap, shoes and stockings were missing. The mud on the soles of her feet seemed to indicate that she had walked barefoot so had lost her shoes and stockings before she got to where her body was found. Her dress was ripped from neck to waist and her hair was matted with blood. Margaret's face was covered in dirt and totally disfigured, her nose almost smashed to a pulp. The rest of her body was covered with grime, especially the lower parts and her knees. There was a wound in the right hip, marks and scratches on the right thigh and several wounds to the inside of the thigh. Above the pubic bone there were marks of extreme violence some extending upwards about five inches. On medical examination of the body by Dr Rayne he concluded that some of the injuries had been caused by using an elbow and feet, others with a knife. Extreme violence had been used to rape Margaret and she had suffered a horrific death. At the inquest Dr Rayne stated that he had never seen such mutilation on a human body except by a machine.

Witnesses had seen Margaret with a man called George Vass. Vass was nineteen and the son of a cab driver. He had been seen dragging a woman by the hair and one arm up Darn Crook. Three of the witnesses, Buckam, Nesbitt and Gillespie thought that the woman looked drunk. They watched Vass throw the

Situated behind what is now Chinatown, a part of the remaining ruins of the West Walls in 2003. The author

Westgate, with the Northern Goldsmith's building on the corner of Clayton Street in 2003. The area looking very different now to when Vass was escorted to the Westgate police station here in 1863. The author

woman to the ground. She was screaming while Vass raped her. The men turned away and went about their business. Why any of these witnesses did not intervene is beyond comprehension. Perhaps because they thought the woman was drunk so therefore she deserved all she got. Vass, meanwhile, was not content with merely violently assaulting his victim, he then proceeded to stab and kick the defenceless woman to death.

The police arrested George Vass in his father's house in Stowell Street. His clothing was found to be bloodstained and he had a knife on his person. Vass was charged with murder and sent to trial. At the Assizes, Mr Blackwell, who was defending Vass, said that his client had ravished 'the poor unfortunate woman' but had not murdered her.

Vass was found guilty of the wilful murder of Margaret Docherty and sentenced to death. His public execution was carried out by Thomas Askern at the corner of the Newcastle gaol facing the Arcade steps.

CHAPTER 18

A Violent Arrest
1863

Mr Eustace, a shoemaker, lived in one room with his family which consisted of his wife, sister-in-law and his three children, Jane, Thomas and Michael. The version of events on the morning of Sunday, 14 June at about four o'clock related by Mr Eustace were that he was sitting with his wife in front of the dying embers of the fire. The rest of the family was asleep except for Michael, who was just preparing to go to bed. There was a noise in the out of doors passage and Michael ran to the window and put his head out. He then left the room and was away for about five minutes. When he returned he locked the door and went to bed. Mr and Mrs Eustace sat talking for another fifteen minutes or so when there was a knock and a man's voice shouting to them to open the door. Mr Eustace refused because of the late hour. There was another knock and Mr Eustace shouted to come back at a reasonable hour. Suddenly the door burst open with the nails holding the bolt being pushed out and landing on the floor. The three men that burst in were policemen. The first into the room was Caseley followed by Vardy and then Taylor, all three had their batons drawn. Mr Eustace asked them what they wanted and Caseley struck him with his baton, knocking him to the floor. Mrs Eustace begged him not to hurt her husband. Mrs Eustace's sister and Jane awoke and began screaming, they were both pushed against a wall. Michael was lying on a bed on the floor. As Thomas got out of his bed one of the men struck him also. Michael then arose, dressed in his nightshirt. As he did so the three policemen closed in on him. Mr and Mrs Eustace saw the batons rising and falling on their son but could do nothing to prevent him being injured. They could not see how many blows were struck or by whom. Michael was twenty-four and a slightly built young man.

The Nag's Head, *one of the many old inns of Newcastle that have been demolished.* Author's collection

Caseley took hold of Michael by his shirt and he sat him on a stool beside the fire. Blood was oozing from Michael's head and it was obvious that he was badly injured. He shouted to his mother to fetch a doctor. Caseley said to him 'Yes you b...... I'll get you a doctor.' Then, hardly giving Michael time to don his trousers, the policemen took him away. Mr Eustace went to the police station the following day and Michael was returned to his parents but within twenty-four hours he was dead. On examination of the body by Dr Raine it was found there was a wound behind the left ear but the cause of death was a severe wound to his left temple.

The version given by the three constables on the event differed from that of Mr Eustace. They stated that Michael had been in a public house on Saturday night and when he headed for home a row had broken out in Silver Street. Michael had been drunk and disorderly and had been throwing stones in the street and that was why they had arrested him. They stated that they had knocked on the door and been invited in. When they had entered Michael was brandishing a poker, Mr Eustace a coal-rake and Thomas had some other sort of a weapon. Vardy had a large bruise on his arm and said that Michael had hit him with the poker so Taylor had hit Michael with his baton to stop him using the poker again and that was the only blow struck by the police. Mr Eustace had a bruise where he said he had been hit by Caseley's baton. Caseley said the wound had occurred when the old man had fallen over a shoemaker's stool.

With this conflicting evidence the jury had to give the case some deep thought. They had to decide whether the police's actions were within the law. There was no doubt that Michael had been drunk and disorderly and throwing stones, but, first, why did the arrest not take place immediately instead of a few hours later? The second point was that the damaged lock on the door was proof that the police had not been invited but had broken in to the Eustace's home. Also the police said they had only struck one blow but Michael had two wounds to his head. The jury stated that, although they thought the arrest in itself was legal, they did not think that there was enough of a threat to the three constables from Michael, even if he had struck Vardy first, for the excessive violence on Taylor's part. The jury summed up by saying that if the blow from Taylor was given with no provocation at all then he would be guilty of murder. They believed, however, that there had been provocation so found Taylor guilty of manslaughter. He was sentenced to three months imprisonment.

CHAPTER 19

Helpless Victims
1859–98

The abject poverty of the working classes meant that the arrival of a new baby was often a burden rather than a joy. A family whose meagre wages did not stretch to feed the mouths they already had would not welcome another. Parents who spent their money on alcohol usually neglected the children they already had and would certainly not give up the habit for another addition. Unmarried girls were often in service. If they had a baby they would lose their employment and their only source of income so could not afford to bring up a child. These facts contributed to the high death rate of newborn and very young babies. Women's apparel made it comparatively easy to hide pregnancy. A newborn could be suffocated or left to bleed to death and the body disposed of without anyone being any the wiser. The other way to dispose of an unwanted burden was abortion. These would often be carried out by someone with little or no medical knowledge and in extremely unhygienic conditions.

19.1 Winlaton 1859:

Elizabeth Hall was twenty-four and lived in as a servant to Mr Grainger, a builder in Newcastle. Her parents lived at Winlaton. On 1 May 1858 Elizabeth met Gloster Smith who was a school master at Winlaton National School. They began seeing each

A nineteenth century sketch of a neglected child. Author's collection

other and Smith took Elizabeth to the Durham Regatta. On heading home they missed the train and did not arrive back in Newcastle until midnight. Suspicion of improper behaviour was aroused and Elizabeth's mother took her daughter to task but Elizabeth insisted that nothing had taken place. Shortly afterwards Elizabeth left her employment and returned home. Smith kept calling on Elizabeth and it made Mrs Hall uneasy so on 1 January of 1859 she sent her daughter to stay with an aunt, Mrs Coombes, at Hopetown near Darlington. Elizabeth left her aunt's house to go to Newcastle, supposedly to look for employment. She had asked her aunt not to tell her father about the first trip. A week later she made a second trip and called in to see her parents on the way back to Hopetown. On Saturday, 29 January Elizabeth made a third journey to Newcastle. She arrived back at Darlington at 6.30 in the evening complaining that she felt very tired and that she had a lot of pain in the lower part of her body. The following day Elizabeth was very ill but refused medical attention. Eventually Mrs Coombes called in Dr JR Fothergill. Just before the doctor arrived, Elizabeth confessed to her aunt that she had had a miscarriage and had burnt the foetus. The doctor attended and for a few days Elizabeth seemed to improve. On the following Saturday she took a turn for the worst and Dr Clarkson was called in to consult with Dr Fothergill but there was nothing the medical men could do for Elizabeth and she died on Monday, 7 February. The post mortem was carried out by the two doctors that had attended Elizabeth and Dr Nichol. Their findings were that poisoning had taken place and her death was due to violence being used to procure an abortion.

Gloster Smith was arrested on suspicion of procuring or performing an abortion which causied Elizabeth's death. At the inquest letters were produced. One had been delivered to Mr Hall for Elizabeth just before she had gone to stay with her aunt. The letter was anonymous and said that no more meetings at night should take place as they were being watched. Elizabeth was to go to the place as she had been instructed and the writer would pay all expenses. The other letters had been written by Elizabeth and were amongst her possessions. They were love letters to someone but there was no name on any of them. The jury found that that there was no factual evidence to link Gloster Smith to the abortion and he was released without charge.

19.2 Newcastle, 1866:

An inquest was held at the dead house in Newcastle on the body of a newborn male infant. Robert Kirkland had been returning from work on Saturday afternoon at about 2.10 pm. He was on the road leading from Westmorland Road leading to Elswick Dene. At the side of the road in a cart rut he noticed a brown paper parcel tied up with thread. On closer inspection he saw a tiny human foot protruding from the paper. Kirkland alerted the police and the body was removed to the dead house. On the baby's head there were marks of violence. The umbilical cord had not been tied and so the infant had bled to death. The mother was not traced so the verdict was 'that the child had been found in a cart rut but how it came there and how its death was caused there was insufficient evidence to show.'

19.3 Elswick, 1870:

On 21 May James Oliver, thirty-five, was charged with committing a rape on Mary Fagan who was just sixteen. Mary had been a servant to Oliver and his wife for four months at their house in East Terrace, Elswick. The family employed other girls in the house and they also had a small shop. There were five rooms in the house. Mary slept in the kitchen with the Oliver's two small boys. Mr and Mrs Oliver slept in the shop and the other girls occupied the remaining rooms.

At 11 pm on Monday Mary had just put the boys to bed and then had gone into the shop. Oliver grabbed hold of Mary and tried to drag her onto the bed but she screamed. Oliver put his coat on and left the house. Two of the girls employed by the family sat with Mary until about 2 am when Oliver returned home. Oliver told Mary to go and bring one of the children into his bedroom. She did as she was asked and then went to her own bed. Mary was woken by Oliver in her bed beside her. She tried to scream but he put his hand over her mouth and forced himself upon her. Mrs Oliver had heard noises and

A 1914 sketch by Robert JS Bertram showing Elswick works. Author's collection

knew something was not right. She entered the kitchen and seeing what her husband was doing she picked up the coal-rake and hit him twice with it.

At the inquest into Oliver's conduct, Inspector George Tunnard stated that at four in the morning Mary and another two women came into Westgate police station and told him of the offence. Tunnard went to the house and arrested Oliver. Dr Hume was called in to examine Mary but could find nothing to show that a rape had taken place. However, Mrs Oliver had seen her husband in bed with Mary so was a key witness. Mary stated that prior to the attack Oliver had, on several occasions, offered her money but had never tried to take liberties with her. The magistrate dealt with the case as aggravated assault rather than rape and sentenced Oliver to six months hard labour. Would the sentence have been more severe had Mary been of the upper class rather than a mere servant?

19.4 Tynemouth, 1898:
In March of 1898 an inquest was held into the death of Albert Edward Cope aged five months. The family lived at 16 Percy Street in Tynemouth. The father, John Cope, was an army

pensioner and there were four other children besides Albert.
The other children's ages were six, five, three and two. The
mother told the court that Albert had never been a healthy
baby but he became seriously ill so she sent for a doctor. Dr
Bramwell attended Albert on the Friday night but the baby
died the following morning. Dr Bramwell told the court that
Albert had died from insufficient nourishment and improper
feeding. Mrs Cope said that she had fed the baby on arrowroot
biscuits and her own milk. Her husband had been out of work
for five months due to the strike and had only resumed work
at Christmas. They still had arrears of rent to pay off. When
asked what money she had coming in, Mrs Cope said that her
husband had a pension of 1s 1d (about 6p) a day and since
Christmas had a weekly wage of 21s. (£1.5p) The Deputy
Coroner told Mrs Cope that, while she might not be well off,
she had enough money coming in to feed her children
properly. He added that he thought Mrs Cope had acted in
ignorance which was common in the poorer classes. Dr
Bramwell told the court that the family was respectable. The
jury found that the child had died from insufficient
nourishment and improper food administered in ignorance
and Mrs Cope was released without charge.

CHAPTER 20

Confession of a Child Killer
1866

Carr Hill was once a small village more or less isolated from Felling and Gateshead. The village had its share of industry including a glass works.

On 13 April 1866 Sarah Melvin, a little girl described as being five or six-years-old, was skipping along in front of her parents at Carr Hill. Sarah's father was a hawker and the family lived at the Blue Quarries. It was about 2.30 on a Friday afternoon when the child was abducted while out of her parent's sight.

The same night Joseph Burns and his wife were proceeding from Carr Hill to Felling when they saw what looked like a sleeping child behind a wall at the side of the road. On closer inspection they were horrified at what they found. It was a little girl and by her terrible injuries it was obvious that she was dead. The lower part of her body was covered in blood and terribly mutilated. The police were alerted and investigations were carried out but for two months the circumstances surrounding her abduction and death remained a mystery.

In June of the same year Cuthbert Rodham Carr gave himself up to the Gateshead police and confessed to being the murderer of Sarah Melvin. Carr was eighteen and lived on a farm near to where the abduction of Sarah had taken place. Carr's father and brother had bound him to an apprenticeship at the glass works, a job which he apparently loathed and his anger at them was the reason he gave for abducting Sarah.

Carr's confession must have turned the stomachs of all who heard it. His story changed slightly towards the end of his statement but he began by saying that he had seen Sarah coming down the road ahead of her parents so he took hold of her and carried her away. The little girl was so frightened she did not cry out or speak at all. Carr carried her into a nearby stable and up the ladder into the loft. Sarah then shouted for her mother so Carr choked her. He then put her under the hay to keep her warm. At about 6.30 pm Carr got a piece of twine about a yard (1 metre) long and split it down its length. He tied one piece of the twine around the child's neck and tied her wrists with the other. Carr said that she already had a lump on her neck and may have been already dead but he was not sure. He then went down the loft ladder and looked out of the stable door. Two women were walking down the road one of whom was a neighbour, Catherine Forster, the other lived beside Felling station. Carr left the stable and walked up the road to where the gate posts were but saw no one else. He waited about five minutes and then saw the two women coming back the other way along the road. They were singing and just ignored Carr. He went into his house. By this time it was about 8 pm. Carr's sister always locked the stable door at night and left the key upon the chimney in the house. When she had done so, Carr took the key and let himself back in to the stable. He carried the body outside and as someone approached he threw it over a wall. When the people had passed by, Carr took Sarah's body on to the road and tried to pick the hay out of her hair. The hay was sticking to her hair because it was wet with water that had come from her mouth. He heard someone else coming so dropped Sarah's body over another wall and then went back into his house. Coming out of the house again Carr intended to take the body to the quarry but as he walked up Split Crow Lane, which was at the back of his house, he saw the child's parents. They were scolding one another, perhaps blaming each other for their daughter being lost. Carr walked past them and up Williamson's Road. He waited a few minutes until the parents had moved further away but before he could get to Sarah somebody else came down the road. Carr then went into his house and to bed. He arose at 4 am and realised the child's body had been found and taken away because there was a policeman and two other men sitting on the wall at the spot he had thrown the body.

Carr was asked if he had used a knife on the lower body of the child. His answer was that he had not used a knife he had torn her with his fingers. Blood saturated the hay around her so he burnt it. He had also removed the twine and burnt that. Carr then admitted that he had choked Sarah and had listened to her gasping for breath for about ten minutes until she died.

Carr was remanded in custody to be visited by gentlemen of the medical profession to determine the state of his mind. He was generally considered by the neighbours to be of weak intellect.

On 10 December Carr stood trial before Justice Lush. When asked how he pleaded to the charge of murder, Carr answered 'Guilty'. Justice Lush asked the prisoner if he understood what he was pleading guilty to. It was explained to Carr that if his plea was guilty there would be no choice but to sentence him to be hanged. If he pleaded not guilty there may be a chance of the lesser charge of manslaughter or even a reprieve. Carr insisted on pleading guilty.

Two doctors were then called to give evidence. The first was Dr Smith who was a surgeon at Sedgefield Lunatic Asylum. He had seen Carr frequently since his committal in June. In Dr Smith's opinion Carr was of unsound mind and not fit to plead. Dr Shaw was a surgeon who practiced at Durham. He

Sedgefield Lunatic asylum in the early twentieth century. Cuthbert Carr was incarcerated here at Her Majesty's Pleasure. Author's collection

THE WINTERTON SECTION, SEDGEFIELD ASYLUM. No 299.

had visited Carr nearly every day since he had been in custody. Dr Shaw's stated that in his opinion Carr was an imbecile and that his imbecility was on the increase. He agreed with Dr Smith that Carr was not fit to plead. Justice Lush then ordered that Carr be kept in strict custody at Her Majesty's Pleasure.

CHAPTER 21

An Unexplained Death
1869

On 16 April a small boy playing beside the Tyne at Scotswood, near to the suspension bridge, saw a body floating on the water. On raising the alarm the body was recovered and identified as twenty-one-year-old John Thomas Mowbray who had worked as a clerk for Mr Beale of Gateshead. There was an abrasion on Mowbray's right temple and a handkerchief was tied with one knot around his neck. On his person there was nothing except for a few coppers.

On tracing Mowbray's movements prior to death it was ascertained that he had left his father's house in Grainger Street on Saturday, 27 March at about 9 pm in the company of another man, Charles Thompson. Mowbray's father, Robert, said that his son had been carrying a watch and

Looking across the Tyne to Newcastle from the Rope Walk in Gateshead, 1819.
Author's collection

chain that had been bought from Mr Potts of Nun Street, a locket bought from Mr Lister and about £2.10s (£2.50) in money. The two men had walked for a short distance through the town of Newcastle and had then stopped for a couple of drinks at *Charlton's* beerhouse in Drury Lane. Thompson and Mowbray had parted company at the bottom of Northumberland Street a little after ten that night. Mowbray was next seen by Mary Ann Lowe on the morning of the following day, which was Easter Sunday, at Mrs Crowther's on Waterloo Street. He had both his breakfast and dinner on the premises and left at about 6.30 pm. Mowbray had a small amount of whisky with his dinner. He told Mary Ann that he was going to the Durham races on Monday and might return to Mrs Crowther's house on the Monday night. Mowbray was not seen again until his body was fished out of the river. Mary thought Mowbray had little money left after paying for his food and drink. Mrs Crowther said the young man had told her he had left his watch at home as he was on a spree.

Grainger Street in the nineteenth century, where Thomas Mowbray lived. Author's collection

At the inquest the medical examiner said that, except for the small abrasion on the temple, there were no other signs of violence and in his opinion the handkerchief was probably tied around Mowbray's neck for warmth, nothing more sinister. He had been in the water for about three weeks and had met his death by drowning. The watch, chain and locket were never found, neither in Mowbray's house nor anywhere else.

The jury brought in a verdict of 'Found dead, but how or by what means there was insufficient evidence to show.'

CHAPTER 22

A Tragedy in Blenheim Street
1870

William Walton, a fifty-five-year-old labourer and his wife, Ann, also fifty-five, lived in a two-roomed, underground cellar at 92 Blenheim Street in Newcastle. The couple had only married in August of 1869 but had lived in the same house for twelve years previously as man and wife. Before meeting Walton, Ann had been married twice, once to a man named Black to whom she had one daughter, Jane. She then married George Reed to whom she had another four children. She had been left a widow. All these five children were now grown up. She and Walton had one child, Annie, who was twelve. Living with them as a lodger was Fredrick Atkins. Atkins was aged twenty-five and worked as a labourer at the Newcastle Central Railway Station.

Walton, who was known as a sober and responsible man, had been out of work for some considerable time due to illness and had become very despondent. Circumstances became so bad that he was compelled to apply to the Guardians for relief and they had been giving him 4s 6d (23p) for the last four weeks. During this time his daughter heard him muttering to

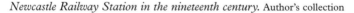

Newcastle Railway Station in the nineteenth century. Author's collection

himself uttering threats against some unknown person. He also began quarreling with his wife over trivial things.

On Sunday night, 6 March one of Ann's sons paid a visit and Walton seemed to be more cheerful. On the Monday morning Walton had risen from bed about eight and had a cigarette. About nine the same morning Ann sent their daughter to Malborough Street on an errand. What seemed to be a normal morning for the family changed in the blink of an eye.

No sooner had Annie left the house when Walton produced a razor and inflicted a deadly wound to his wife's throat. He then armed himself with a pair of fire tongs and went to the bedroom of their lodger. Atkins was fast asleep as he had worked night-shift and had returned home at six that morning. Walton struck Atkins a violent blow to his head. The startled man, despite his wound, jumped from the bed and tried to grapple the fire-tongs from Walton's grasp. It was a desperate struggle in which Walton managed to reign another few blows on his victim. While the two were fighting Annie returned from her errand. On seeing her mother lying dead in the kitchen and the two men fighting she ran out of the house to get her half-sister, Jane Reed, who was Ann's eldest daughter. Jane was in service to Mrs Brown who was the publican of the *Woolpack Inn* in Marlborough Street.

Atkins eventually managed to wrest the fire-tongs from Walton's grasp. From somewhere in his clothing, Walton produced another razor and lunged at Atkins with it. He succeeded in inflicting two large wounds in Atkins' neck and also cut his wrists as the man tried to protect himself against the lethal weapon. Somehow Atkins managed to take the razor from Walton and run upstairs to a provision shop that was on the corner of Blenheim and Churchill Streets immediately above the cellars. Appearing from nowhere, covered in blood and with an open razor in his hand, Atkins must have presented a terrifying sight. He was eventually able to catch his breath and relate what had happened.

Someone went to the Westgate police station to raise the alarm. Sergeant Tunnah and Sergeant Johnson proceeded to the house. Entering the blood-splashed kitchen they found Mrs Walton lying behind the door. In the room where the two men had struggled Walton was lying on his back in a pool of warm blood. There was a deep, long gash to his throat which had been inflicted with such force as to almost sever his head. It would appear that as soon as Atkins had escaped, Walton had procured another razor and had taken his own life. Dr's Stainthorpe and Hume were called but Mr and Mrs Walton were beyond their help.

As crowds collected around the house there was speculation as to the reason for Walton to kill his wife and to try and kill Atkins. It was thought by some that Walton was jealous of the lodger. At the inquest this theory was introduced but there were no grounds to show that his wife had been unfaithful. It was decided that Walton had committed the acts whilst of unsound mind due to his depression at being out of work.

Thomas Atkins had suffered a severe compound fracture of the skull, three other smaller wounds to his head, cuts to his neck and other lacerations. He was not expected to survive but, after treatment taking a few months, he pulled through.

It was Annie Walton's twelfth birthday when the tragic events took place. She went to stay with one of her half-brothers who lived in Newcastle. None of the family was in a position to take her in indefinitely so a subscription was raised to pay for her keep until she was old enough to work.

Walton had committed *felo de se* so could not be buried in consecrated ground. As law demanded he was buried without service at the crossroads between Stepney Lane and Shieldfield.

CHAPTER 23

Trivial Incidents
1870–72

23.1 A Blow from a Fist, 1870:

On Saturday, 7 May in the bar of Robert Cowens in Mill House Lane, Bentinck there were about ten men forming two groups standing in front of the counter. In one group was Alexander Ross who was fifty-eight and in the other Thomas Lewthwaite who was twenty-four, both men worked as shoemakers. Ross was married and lived in Portland Street. Lewthwaite was single and lodged in the same street. The two men began a heated argument about some trivial matter. Lewthwaite lost his temper and struck the older man with his fist. The blow caught Ross on his jugular vein and he was knocked to the floor. Lewthwaite then left the building. Cowens assisted Ross into a back room. The landlord could see the man was in a bad way so sent for a doctor. Dr Angus arrived within a very short time but he was too late, Ross was dead. On asserting the cause of death the doctor said that even if he had been on the premises when the injury was afflicted his services would have been of no avail. Ross was taken to his own house to await burial.

The police were notified and went to look for Lewthwaite but did not find him at his lodgings. That evening at about 7.30 Lewthwaite gave himself up at the Manors police station. On Monday an inquest was held at the *Bellgrave Hotel* in North Mill Lane. Ross' wife said that her husband would have been fifty-nine on 22 May if he had lived. She said that prior to this incident there had been no bad feeling between the two men. The witnesses that were in the bar on the Saturday night all agreed that the death had been the result of an accident caused by larking about. The jury agreed that there was no wilful intention involved and returned a verdict of manslaughter against Lewthwaite.

23.2 A Blow from a Rifle Butt, 1870:

At about 6.30 on the evening of Friday, 31 December Anthony Reay and his wife, Margaret, were walking up Barrack Road. As they neared the gates of Thompson and Boyd's factory a man was walking towards them on the same side of the road. Over the man's shoulder were a carpet-bag and a carbine rifle. As they went to pass each other the carpet bag struck Reay on the shoulder. Words passed between the two men and the altercation resulted in Reay being struck on the forehead by the carbine. The blow knocked him to the ground and his wife could see that he was badly injured. Reay was taken to the infirmary where some pieces of bone were removed from the wound. Once the wound had been treated he was sent home. His condition steadily worsened and he died on 11 January at his house at 24 Hindhaugh Street. The cause of death was established as a severely fractured skull inflicted by a heavy blow with a blunt instrument, in this case, the rifle.

An inquest was held on 13 January at the house of Mr Peter Turnbull at the *Black Bull Inn* in Barrack Road. Reay was twenty-nine and worked as an engine-fitter for Leadicote Rivetting Works at Gateshead. Before he died he had made a statement as to what had happened on the 31 December. Reay said he knew the man that had bumped into him but only by sight. He had since learned that the man's name was Thomas Brown. On the evening in question Reay stated that when Brown had bumped against him with the carpet-bag he had asked him what the hell he thought he was doing. Brown had replied with a nasty remark so Reay had walked up to him in a threatening manner. Brown had put his tools and the gun on the ground. Reay began to take his jacket off ready for a fight but his wife intervened. Brown said that he would rather buy Reay a glass of ale than fight him. The apology accepted Reay put his jacket back on and turned away to go home with his wife. Suddenly he felt a sharp blow to his forehead and he fell to the ground in great pain. His wife had him taken to the infirmary where his wound was treated. Reay said he was then sent home and had not been able to leave his bed since the incident. He also said that he was not drunk having had only five or six glasses of ale.

Newcastle Infirmary in 1855. Reay's wound was treated here and he was then sent home. Author's collection

Margaret Reay made a statement saying that her husband had been slightly drunk when the incident occurred. She pointed out that the footpath they had been walking on was wide enough for four or five people to pass each other without bumping into anybody. When Brown hit her husband with the rifle Margaret retaliated by hitting Brown with a small breakfast-can she had in her hand. Brown then picked up his bag and walked away. Although the altercation had nearly come to blows Margaret could see no reason for Brown to have hit her husband with the gun as the two men seemed to have solved their differences and her husband was about to walk away.

Another witness was called, a man by the name of Smith. He stated that he had been working with Brown on that fateful day. They had been putting up a shed at Heathery Shank farm. When they had finished they headed home stopping to have a few drinks on the way. As they were going along Barrack Road Smith had stopped to talk to an acquaintance outside the *General Moor* and Brown had walked on. Smith heard voices raised in argument and as he approached the source he saw Brown hit Reay with the rifle. Brown was a volunteer in Captain Boyd's division of the Gateshead Corps and he had borrowed the rifle to put in some target practice. The rifle had since been returned to the Corp's headquarters.

It was established that Brown was of good character and that he had been employed at Thompson and Boyd's works for about ten years. On these merits the jury brought in a verdict of manslaughter rather than murder.

This tragedy took place on New Years Eve and it is likely that these two men had had more to drink than they admitted to. The events that took place show clearly how a trivial incident can have such dire consequences.

23.3 Death by Drowning, 1872:

Mary Copperthwaite, who was described as an 'unfortunate', had met Louis Johann Frederick Richenback, a German, at the *Black Swan Inn* at Wapping at about five o'clock on the evening of 1 January. They drank two bottles of ginger beer and then left the inn. As the couple walked out into the street William James approached them and, without a word spoken and with no apparent reason, pulled the cigar from Richenback's mouth. On Rickenback asking for the cigar to be returned James ignored the request and instead punched him knocking him to the ground. Richenback stood up and after handing Mary his watch, he took off his hat and coat ready to defend himself against his aggressor. Another man, Nesbitt, approached and before Richenback knew what was happening he received a punch from the second man. Mary grabbed Richenback by the shoulders and pushed him through the door of a lodging house that had previously been the *Half Moon Inn.* The other two men followed them in and shouting abuse began throwing plates at their victim. James and Nesbitt then began thrashing the defenceless man using foul language towards him at the same time. Mary tried to stop the two men but James pushed her aside and then threatened to stab Richenback. A sister to the lodging house keeper came into the room to see what the noise was. James shouted at her that he would stab her if she interfered. She lifted a chair to try and hit James but he stopped her and, still hurling verbal abuse, continued punching Richenback. Mrs Julien, the owner of the house, then entered the room and on seeing what was happening lifted a bottle and hit Mary over the head and pushed her out of the door. The men then got the same treatment. Richenback was pushed out of a side door that led into a lane. His two tormentors had been evicted through the front door. As James began to walk down the street he spotted his victim in the lane. Giving a loud scream James ran towards him. Richenback tried to get away by running up the Mission Ship stairs but James caught up with him, pulled him back down the stairs and pushed him into the river. By this time it was early on the morning of 2 January and there were a number of people standing about. Mary, who had followed the men, shouted for someone to help the drowning man. One of the spectators answered with 'He's only a Prussian, let him go.' Nesbitt must have had an attack of conscience because he pulled off his coat ready to jump into the river but someone grabbed him and stopped him doing so. Rickenback's body was recovered from the river later that day. On medical examination it was determined that he had died due to drowning. Rather oddly the surgeon, Dr Coward, said he found no marks of violence on the body.

James and Nesbitt were charged with wilful murder and the initial trial was held at the *Marine Hotel* on Ocean Road, South Shields. Mrs Julien was called as a witness and she related what had taken place in her lodging house adding that both James and Nesbitt were very violent. Other witnesses included Mary, a boatman and a little girl who had all seen James push Rickenback into the river. The coroner decided there was no evidence against Nesbitt for the murder so he was released without charge. James was committed for trial at the Assizes. He narrowly escaped the death sentence as the jury found him guilty of manslaughter rather than murder. He was sentenced to twenty years penal servitude. Today this behavior, which was clearly a racist attack, would not be tolerated and James would have been found guilty of murder. However the sentence James received would probably not have been much different today.

The Marine Hotel *where the initial trial of James and Nesbitt was held.* The author

CHAPTER 24

For Love or Money?
1875

In 1873 Richard Charlton was a farm labourer working for Mr William Robson on a large farm called Gardner's House, near Dinnington. While working there he met Sarah Duxfield Fenwick, the sister of his employer's wife. The two soon became a couple and decided to marry. Sarah had been left £300 when her father died (a considerable sum of money at that time) and her family believed that Richard was only after the inheritance. Sarah, however, did not listen to her family's warnings and on 12 May, 1873 the couple married in secret without telling anyone until after the event. They moved to a house at Horton Grange but, after a short time, moved back to Dinnington. Charlton took employment as a hand for Mr Taylor at a farm two miles from Dinnington.

It did not turn out to be a marriage made in heaven as the couple constantly argued over Sarah's money. When Sarah fell pregnant the situation became worse and her husband became tyrannical and cruel towards her. Arrangements had been made for Sarah to have her baby at Gardner's House where her sister, Ann, would be able to look after her. On 7 April 1875, a few days after moving into the farm, Sarah gave birth to a boy. Charlton visited Sarah after the birth and they argued about a name for their son. Ann took part in the argument and Charlton threatened to hit her saying that she was turning his wife against him. After that he visited Sarah at regular intervals asking her to return to him but she always

Newcastle in 1875. Author's collection

refused. Early on the morning of 5 June Charlton went to see Sarah but left when William told him that she was not yet up. Charlton returned that afternoon. Sarah came into the kitchen just as her husband arrived and he asked her if she would return to him. She adamantly refused. Ann was in the parlour with another of Sarah's sisters, Margaret Bennet, and a friend, Jane Robinson. Ann heard the voices raised in anger and went into the kitchen to see what was going on. When she saw the couple arguing Ann told Sarah to open the door to see Charlton out. Charlton accused Ann of making mischief. Ann once again told Sarah to open the door but, at this, Charlton grabbed Sarah's arm, took a revolver from his pocket and fired twice at Sarah's head. He then turned the weapon on Ann. The bullet glanced along Ann's cheek and although she felt pain she was able to run away. Sarah was not so lucky. She was lying on the floor moaning in agony. Jane Robinson had been holding Sarah's son and in fear of the baby's life and her own she ran outside. Ann took refuge in the pantry where Margaret was already crouched in terror. Charlton fired again and a bullet hit Margaret Bennet. With strength born from fear Ann managed to put her full force against the door and hold it closed as Charlton rushed at it. He then started firing at the door but the wood was solid and the bullets did not pass through. Charlton then seemed to become even more enraged and made another rush at the door succeeding in pushing it partially open. Ann, in trying to push the door shut again disclosed a portion of her hand. Charlton took advantage and fired, the bullet slit Ann's thumb, passed through the top of her hand and fell to the floor. All went quiet for a minute or so and then Charlton appeared outside at the pantry window. He fired through the glass but his aim was erratic and he missed the two women. Charlton made his way back round the building and re-entered the house. Ann heard another shot and then an eerie silence. After what must have seemed like an eternity Ann ventured out from the pantry. Charlton was lying, motionless, on the floor beside Sarah. One of the Robson's farm labourers, Bartholomew Watson, sent for assistance and then entered the house. Jane Robinson had returned to the house by this time so she and Watson put

Sarah on the sofa. They then brought a mattress from a bedroom into the kitchen and laid Charlton on it until the police and two doctors arrived. Dr Jamieson from Ponteland and Dr Heath of Newcastle thought that Charlton would not survive the journey to the Newcastle Infirmary so he was taken to his own house under police guard. He had shot himself through the cheek. Ann's injuries were serious but not life threatening. Margaret later died from her injuries. Sarah died the following day but her husband survived. It would have perhaps have been better for him if his suicide attempt had been successful. The bullet had stayed lodged within his head and he was left paralysed down his left side. He recovered enough to eventually stand trial on 2 December at Northumberland Assizes. It came to light that Charlton had purchased the five chamber revolver from a pawnshop in Newcastle the day before the shootings. It was also clear by the amount of bullets that had been fired that he had re-loaded the revolver. Charlton's defence tried to plead insanity but the jury found that his actions had been premeditated and calculating. They found him guilty of wilful murder and he was sentenced to death. A petition was drawn up and signed by numerous influential people requesting a reprieve. The grounds for the petition were that Charlton had considerable provocation and that provocation had driven him to insanity. The reprieve was denied and Richard Charlton was hanged by William Marwood at Morpeth gaol on the morning of 23 December, 1875. This was the first private execution to be carried out at Morpeth and the last public execution there had been nearly thirty years previously on 17 March 1847.

Before his death Charlton asked his brother, Joseph, to take care of the child, which he agreed to do. The child would benefit from the sale of the furniture that was in the Charlton's house and about £10 that had belonged to his father. There was also about £240 of his mother's money still in a Newcastle bank. No consolation for losing both parents in such tragic circumstances.

CHAPTER 25

A Bad End to a Good Day
1875

William Wood, George Hunter, Robert Schooler and Thomas Arnott all resided just outside the village of Dinnington and worked in the local collieries. On 9 December 1875 they headed out of Dinnington for an afternoon's shooting. Wood was the only one of the four without a gun. When it began to get dark at about 5.30, Wood, Hunter and Arnott decided to have a few jars in the *Carrgate Inn* at the low end of Dinnington. Schooler did not drink so he went to see a friend saying he would call back for his companions later on that night. The three men spent a pleasant evening laughing and joking with the other customers in the public house. Schooler returned and the four friends, along with another two men, Sampson Mead and Thomas Thorn, left the Inn a little after 10 pm and walked towards Dinnington Church. Hunter, Schooler and Arnott had their still loaded guns over their shoulders. The ground was covered with soft snow and Wood was throwing snowballs at Thorn, which was taken in good part. Mead and Thorn came to where they lived and the four friends stopped to say goodnight to them.

As the four friends carried on walking, Schooler and Arnott were some distance in front of the other two. Wood began to throw snowballs at Hunter but he, apparently, was not amused. The two men in the lead heard Hunter shout to Wood that if he did not stop he would fire the gun at him. Wood shouted back to Hunter that he would not do that. Schooler and Arnott then heard a shot. They stopped to see what had happened and Hunter strolled up to them and asked Arnott for his powder flask. They asked Hunter if he had fired at Wood. Hunter replied that he had. They then asked if the shot had hit Wood and Hunter once again replied in the affirmative. Schooler and Arnott, leaving Hunter standing with his gun still in his hand, ran back the way they had come. Wood was lying on the footpath with his chest and the snow beneath covered with his blood. The two men alerted the police and a doctor. When Wood's body was examined by Dr Walker he thought that death must have been instantaneous. Police Constable Davidson took Hunter into custody and had to almost drag him along the road as he seemed dazed and confused.

Hunter stood trial before Baron Bramwell at the Northumberland Assizes held at Newcastle. No one spoke on Hunter's behalf and the evidence of the two witnesses was given clearly. The whole trial lasted less than an hour with the jury finding Hunter guilty of wilful murder but with a recommendation for mercy. Baron Bramwell sentenced Hunter to death but said that the jury's recommendation would be forwarded to the Home Secretary.

The recommendation for mercy was denied and Hunter was hanged by William Marwood on 28 March, 1876 at Morpeth gaol. His body was interred on the north east side of the prison with the coffin end to end with that of Richard Charlton who had been hanged in December of the previous year. Hunter was the last person to be executed at Morpeth and the gaol was closed in 1881.

CHAPTER 26

Anonymous Letters
1894

Mary Ann Marshall, known to her friends as Polly, lived with her parents in Cross Street, Tynemouth. Her favourite haunt was a walking route between Whitley Bay and Tynemouth called the Broadway. The route led to Holy Saviour's Church at Tynemouth which was a meeting place for courting couples. Polly was just seventeen when she met Samuel George Emery. Emery was twenty and a soldier from West Bromwich who was serving as a private in the South Staffordshire Regiment. Polly became smitten with the young man, whether it was for his good looks or the glamour of his uniform, when he was based at Tynemouth Barracks. A soldier's life is never certain and eventually Emery was transferred to Strensall near York. The couple wrote to each other frequently and Polly thought that all was well. What Polly did not know was that Emery had been receiving anonymous letters telling him that Polly was seeing other men behind his back. For a while Emery wrote to Polly even more often pledging his undying love but then suspicion and doubt

The ruins of Tynemouth Priory in the eighteenth century. It was in a nearby field that Mary Ann Marshall met her death at the hands of her jealous lover.
Author's collection

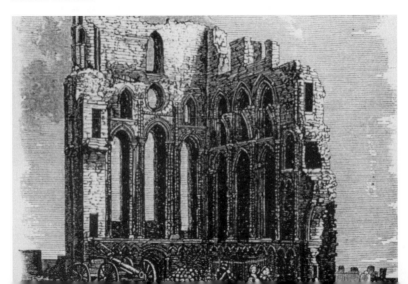

must have crept in. When Polly opened a letter from Emery one day she could not understand what she was reading. It was almost a threat telling her she had better behave or he would arrive when she least expected him.

After receiving another anonymous letter Emery's jealousy got the better of him and on 21 July he went AWOL and jumped on a train to Tynemouth. Polly opened the door to a very upset boyfriend. What was said between the two lovers over the next two days was known only to them. The letters must have been spoken about and Polly would have denied any wrongdoing. She must have thought that Emery believed her and all was well because on 23 July Polly went out to meet Emery again. This was against her father's wishes as he felt she was too young for this serious relationship and certainly too young for marriage.

On that Monday the couple met up and walked together to Holy Saviour's Church. Perhaps the letters were mentioned again and perhaps Polly's pledge of undying love for her young soldier went unheard. Whatever transpired Emery already had murder in mind because that afternoon he had bought a large clasp knife and had even asked the shop owner to sharpen the blade. Under the shadow of the peaceful church of the Holy Saviours, Emery's jealousy turned to rage and, pulling a knife from his pocket, he stabbed wildly at Polly. She held up her arms as she tried to defend herself against his attack but after stabbing her several times on the hands and arms the blade reached its mark and she was stabbed in the throat. There were three men who were witnesses to the attack including Reverend T B Nichols, the vicar of the church, and they all gave chase as Emery sped off. James Gibson, a chemist, managed to get quite close to the fleeing man but Emery turned and threatened him with the knife. Gibson said later that as Emery slashed out with the knife his teeth were clenched and he looked like a mad and desperate man. Emery missed with his wildly directed blow and then turned and ran towards the railway sidings where he was lost from sight.

Emery apparently hid until it was dark and went to the *Crescent Tavern* in Hudson Street. Later that evening he was recognized by two policemen and taken into custody. When he was told Polly was dead he said he was glad. He made a full confession stating that he had intended murder before he left his army camp. Emery stood trial before Justice Charles at the Newcastle Assizes on 20 November, 1894 for Polly's murder. He was found guilty with no recommendation for mercy and sentenced to death. While the young man was waiting for his sentence to be carried out he began to realize that his jealousy had been unfounded and the letters had been the work of a poison pen. He wrote to Polly's father asking forgiveness for what he had done. Assisted by the executioner William Billington, Samuel Emery took his last earthly walk on 11 December, 1894, not on Broadway where he had been so happy, but to the gallows.

Who the letters were written by and for what reason was never discovered but the 'power of the pen' was certainly strong in this case. It took the lives of two young people in their prime.

CHAPTER 27

Beaten with a Coal-rake
1898

Annie Irving was just twenty-seven when she met a violent death. She had come from Dumfries in Scotland a few years previously and moved into 10 Cannon Street in Newcastle. Cannon Street was one of the thoroughfares of Scotswood Road and was near to the *Crooked Billet* public house. Annie lodged in a three roomed downstairs flat with Alexander Thompson, his wife, Jean, and sixteen year-old daughter, May. Annie, by all accounts, got on very well with the family. Alexander Thompson had joined the army when he was seventeen and had seen active service in Afghanistan. On his return to Newcastle about two years later, he had married Jane Robinson, who he called Jean. He worked as a labourer at Sir William Armstrong's works in Newcastle.

Annie had worked since she arrived in Newcastle as a waitress in Mr Winship's cocoa house at East Terrace at the foot of Elswick. She had just changed her job and gone to work at the Electric Lighting Company at Benwell where May Thompson worked. On Saturday afternoons Annie usually accompanied Mrs Thompson and her daughter to the market. One Saturday in March Annie decided not to go to the market as she felt tired. She told Mrs Thompson that she would stay at home in the afternoon to rest and go out that evening instead. Mother and daughter went out at about 3.30 pm leaving Annie sitting reading the paper.

When Mrs Thompson and May returned from the market at around 6 pm they certainly were not prepared for the scene that awaited them. Annie was lying in the passage in a pool of blood. It was obvious by the terrible injuries to her head and face that she was dead. Mrs Thompson ran from the house screaming for help. When the police arrived Annie's body was conveyed to the dead house at St Lawrence where she was examined by Dr Baumgartner, the police surgeon. He found a deep gash on both the front and back of her head and two gashes on her face. The lobe of one of her ears was cut in two and she had other less severe wounds on other parts of her body. The doctor thought that she had been dead some time so the murder must have taken place shortly after Mrs Thompson and May had left the house to go to the market. On searching the house the police found a coal-rake in the kitchen. As testimony to having been used as the murder weapon to beat Annie to death the coal-rake was covered with blood and hair. Blood spattered the walls and floor of the kitchen and passage showing that Annie must have put up a terrific struggle against her assailant before she was finally murdered.

On questioning the neighbours the police spoke to Mrs Claydon, who lived upstairs at number 10. She said she had heard a woman screaming at about 4.30 pm but thought it was Mrs Thompson chastising her daughter so took no notice. She then heard the Thompson's front door slam shut about ten minutes later. Mrs Isabella Jones lived opposite at number 9 Cannon Street. She told the police that she had seen Alexander Thompson come out of number 10 sometime between 4 pm and 5 pm and that he looked as though he had been drinking.

Thompson was found and arrested later that evening but was too drunk to be charged until the following morning. What appeared to be bloodstains were found on his clothes. Thompson was taken before the magistrates several times and on each occasion was remanded to Newcastle gaol while the police searched for further evidence. The reason for the many remands was that there had been two previous murders of young

A sketch of Alexander Thompson at his initial trial for murder. Author's collection women in similar circumstances. One had taken place at Gosforth and one on the Town Moor, both had remained unsolved. The police suspected Thompson of these murders and had been locating different witnesses. Thompson appeared before the magistrates on Monday and was once again remanded while a police line up was arranged for that day. Four witnesses, Brown, Burgam, Jones and Trainer identified Thompson as being the last to be seen with each of the murdered women.

On the Friday following the line up Thompson went to bed in his cell at the usual time. He was kept in an observation cell where a warder would check on him periodically. When the warder did his rounds at midnight he looked through the grating of Thompson's cell and saw that he was in bed. Passing back about ten minutes later, the warder looked in again and saw Thompson had left his bed. The warder waited a few minutes and then became suspicious when he could hear no sound from the cell. The warder did not have access to the cells and had to send for the Chief Warder, Mr Joseph Barlow, to obtain a key. This caused a considerable delay and by the time the cell was unlocked it was too late for Thompson. His body was hanging from the ventilator. A hanky was tied to the grid and then to a towel which was around Thompson's neck. He had strangled himself.

Thompson had written letters to his wife and daughter protesting his innocence and telling them that the witnesses were lying. He also wrote that he wanted to end it all but was being watched too closely. In a letter that Jean had written back to her husband she had written that she believed him to be innocent of all the murders. At the inquest into his death the prosecutor, Mr Edward Clark, stated that perhaps it was fortunate for the public and Thompson that he had used a speedy means to get rid of himself as he would have been charged with all three murders. It was also pointed out that until 1832 *felo de se*, or suicide, was an act of self destruction and the law stated that the body would have been interred at a crossroads. As it was he would be buried with no service read over him.

Did Thompson commit suicide because he was guilty or because he was innocent? No other investigations were carried out so this case remains unproven.

CHAPTER 28

A Crime of Passion
1901

Maggie Ann Whiston had married a ship's steward, Lazare Lieutand, in 1896. They set up home in Newcastle but her husband was away at sea a great deal of the time and after a while Maggie Ann left him. John George Thompson was an engineer and fitter who served his time at Armstrongs in Newcastle. He left the firm and went to sea for a short time but returned to work there in 1894. He was well thought of at the firm and earned good wages.

Maggie Ann was thirty-three and Thompson thirty-eight when the two met just before Easter in 1901. They moved in together at a house in Byker but the arrangement was not a happy one. Thompson left the house and his job and went to London but soon returned to live in Gateshead. Maggie moved to 121 Milling Street with a friend, Ivy Dawson. They had four rooms on the upper floor with an entrance to the front and rear of the house via a staircase.

On Friday, 14 September, Thompson called at Milling Street to speak to Maggie Ann. She took him upstairs and introduced him to her friend. Thompson wanted to speak to Maggie Ann alone but she declined and told him they were going to Newcastle so he would have to leave. The two women went to Newcastle and came across Thompson several times. He did not speak but appeared to be watching and following them. They became nervous and were afraid to return home. Maggie Ann and Ivy wandered around until midnight and then headed home by the Redheugh Bridge. After passing the cattle market they saw no further sign of their stalker.

On the following Monday Maggie Ann and Ivy were at the post office in Gateshead when Thompson approached and said 'I want to speak to you May.' Maggie Ann replied 'I don't want to speak to you and if you will let things drop, I will let

High Street, Gateshead, in 1910. Author's collection

things drop.' Thompson then told her she was a drunken liar and only spoke the truth by accident. He then said something about his mother. Maggie Ann told Thompson to go away. He was white with anger and began making threats towards her. Ivy told him to stop and the two women left the post office and went back to Milling Street. Later that day Maggie Ann and Ivy went to visit Maggie Ann's sister. As they were returning in a tram car they saw Thompson heading towards their house so Maggie Ann crouched down on the floor so he would not see her. They stayed on the tram and went past their stop getting out a little further on hoping that by the time they arrived home Thompson would be gone.

Maggie Ann and Ivy went by Askew Road towards their house. When they reached Milling Street at about 2.30 pm Thompson was standing on the corner. Again he tried to speak to 'May' as he called her. She refused and the two women entered their house, Maggie Ann entering first. As Ivy tried to shut the door Thompson pushed his way in and began to run up the stairs. Ivy managed to grab him by the collar and pull him down. Maggie Ann was still in the passage. Thompson had, at first, run by not seeing her in his rage. Ivy saw something glinting in Thompson's hand and then she heard a shot and realised it was a gun. Maggie Ann did not seem injured at this point but the bullet had actually caught her just under the left arm. Thompson then grabbed her and tried to put the pistol down her collar. Ivy screamed at Maggie Ann to run for her life. Mrs Boyle had opened her door, which was opposite at 122 Milling Street, when the first shot was fired. Maggie Ann broke away from her assailant and ran out to the street and through the opposite door. Ivy shut the door of her house and ran upstairs trembling with shock and fear. She heard two more shots fired and then silence. Ivy ran out and to the police station. When she returned with a policeman and entered Mrs Boyle's house Thompson was sitting on the floor in a pool of blood cradling Maggie Ann in his arms. She was taken to her own house but died soon after. Thompson was arrested and charged with murder.

The trial was held at the Autumn Assizes at Durham before Justice Grantham. There had been another witness to the events on that day besides Ivy and Mrs Boyle. Henry Alder Smith who was a draper's traveler had been selling his goods in Milling Street and had seen Thompson push his way into the house and then follow Maggie Ann as she ran across the street.

Charles Atkinson worked for Mr Mendelssohn in his shop in Blackett Street. The shop was a general dealer and, amongst other goods, sold revolvers. He recognized the revolver that was shown to him as one he had sold but could not remember the customer. Justice Grantham pointed out to Atkinson that he should know what sometimes happened when revolvers were purchased and should be more observant towards his customers in the future. Charles Watson was a gunsmith and stated that Thompson had bought a box of fifty cartridges from him about 1 pm on Monday. The police stated that the

Map showing the location of Blackett Street where John Thompson bought the revolver which he used to shoot Maggie Lieutand. Ordnance Survey, Central Newcastle, 1914

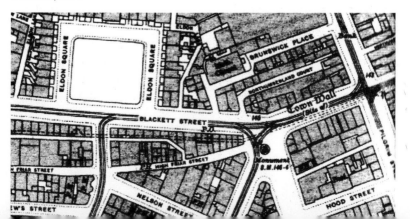

box that they found in Thompson's possession still held forty five cartridges, there were two still in the chamber of the revolver and three had been fired.

Thompson's defence tried to plead insanity but to no avail. Thompson had bought the revolver and cartridges and used them in an obviously pre-meditated act. The charge could not even be reduced to manslaughter because of the circumstances. The jury found Thompson guilty of murder and Justice Grantham sentenced him to death.

On 10 December 1901 John George Thompson was hanged by Thomas Billington, assisted by his brother William, within the confines of Durham gaol.

CHAPTER 29

The Cullercoats' Affair
1901

On 15 November 1901 the Northumberland Assizes resumed at the Moot Hall in Newcastle. On trial before Justice Grantham were John Miller, a travelling hawker, who was sixty-seven and his nephew, John Robert Miller, a travelling musician, who was thirty-one. They were charged with the murder of Joseph Ferguson at 55 Huddleston Road, Cullercoats on the afternoon of 20 September. The victim had died from haemorrhaging caused by eight knife wounds inflicted on him. Joseph Ferguson had married, four years previously, Mrs Miller. She had been the second wife of Mr Miller, the father of the older prisoner so this made Ferguson the step-father of the elder Miller. Ferguson was sixty seven and a merry-go-round proprietor.

On the 20 September the two accused men had gone to a shop in North Shields owned by Mr Purvis. They told Mr Purvis that the younger man was going to sea as a ship's cook

Map showing the location of the Moot Hall where the trial of Joseph and John Miller was held. Ordnance Survey, Newcastle & Gateshead, 1894

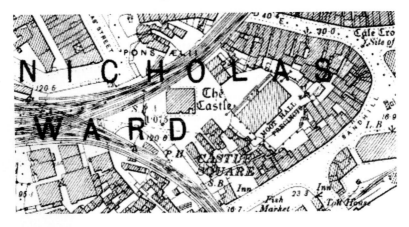

The Moot Hall in 2003. The foundation stone was laid in July 1810 and the building was remodelled in 1875. The building is now used as a criminal court and also a tourist attraction where mock trials are enacted. The author

and they wished to purchase a particular type of knife for his work. They selected a knife, paid for it and left. The men were later seen walking in the direction of Cullercoats. At 3.30 pm a boy, Stephen Oliver saw the two Millers coming out of the *Bay Hotel* and go towards Huddleston Road. Oliver then saw the older of the two men secrete himself in a doorway while the younger man knocked on the door of Ferguson's house. When the door was answered the young man entered and then the older man came out from his hiding place and followed and the door was closed behind them. James Melvin, a grocer, had a shop in Huddleston Street. He also had seen what had taken place at the Ferguson's front door. Other witnesses that had seen the two men throughout the course of the day stated that the younger of the two was staggering drunk.

The house was divided into two flats and the Fergusons' had the upper floor. At the front there was an outer and inner door. There were stairs to the upper flat from the front door and stairs at the back leading down to the rear entrance which opened

A sketch of John Miller and John Robert Miller at the time of their trial. Author's collection

The Bay Hotel *in the early nineteenth century.* Author's collection

onto a back lane. The events that took place immediately afterwards were related by Mrs Ferguson. She told the court that she and her husband had been upstairs in the kitchen when they heard a knock at the door. Ferguson went to answer the knock and two men entered the house. She thought that the last man in bolted the front door behind him. Ferguson was then attacked with a knife by one of the men but it was unclear who the attacker was. The attacker then ran upstairs and showed the terrified woman the knife before throwing the weapon down and leaving by the back stairs. Mrs Ferguson shouted from her upstairs window for a neighbour to get the police. Two neighbours, realizing something was wrong, tried the front door but it was bolted from the inside. They went round to the back of the house and on entering found Ferguson lying dead in the passage. By this time a small crowd had gathered outside. Witnesses saw the elder of the two Millers leaning against a doorway calmly lighting his pipe. There was a patch of blood on his face. The younger Miller was pacing to

The Bay Hotel *in 2002.* Author's collection

Huddleston Road in Cullercoats. Author's collection

and fro looking extremely nervous. Someone shouted to the crowd to hold the two men until the police arrived.

No motive was ever forthcoming for the brutal murder. Each man blamed the other. The younger of the two said that his uncle had placed the knife in his hand and goaded him into the attack. The elder said that if his eyesight had been better he could have stopped the attack being carried out. Both men were found guilty of murder and sentenced to death. It came to light that John Robert had previously spent some time in a lunatic asylum and was not considered completely sane. Letters were sent to the Home Secretary to ask for a reprieve but the request was denied.

The execution of the two men was carried out at Newcastle gaol on 7 December by Thomas Billington and John Ellis. James Billington, Thomas' father, was supposed to carry out the execution but was ill with pneumonia at the time. He died of the illness later that month. This was a private execution and all that could be seen by the public was the black flag being hoisted. This did not deter a crowd of thousands collecting outside the gaol as this was the first double execution in Newcastle for 117 years. It was reported that the elder Miller went to his fate with reasonable calm but John Robert was hysterical until the end.

John Ellis assisted in the execution of the Millers.
Author's collection

CHAPTER 30

Murder of an Innocent at Bill Quay 1902

ary Ina Stewart was one of six children of a widower, James Stewart. On the morning of Saturday, 16 August at about 10.30, seven-year-old Mary left her home at 16 Joel Terrace, Bill Quay with her friend, Geraldine Scott, to visit Mary's uncle, Frederick Stewart. Her uncle lived a short distance away at 8 Gosforth Terrace just over a bank known as Hilly Fields. Mary's father, who was a brickmaker, had gone to work at Hexham. When he returned at about 10.30 in the evening Mary was not in the house. Her father waited a short time and then decided to go to his brother's house in Pelaw to collect her. When James arrived his brother told him that Mary had been there but that he had walked her and her friend part of the way home at about 7.30 pm. James by now was very worried and immediately he reached home he organized a search party.

The search for the little girl continued throughout that night and all of Sunday. They went through the Cat Dene Quarry and searched the grass right up to the water side but there was no trace of the missing child. Wood, Skinner and Co's disused brickyard had already been searched. On Monday, because there had still been no trace of the little girl and because of the abundance of long grass, the yard was searched again more

Hexham, where James Stewart was at work as his daughter was being brutally assaulted and murdered. Author's collection

thoroughly. Eventually, Mary's body was found near a wooden wall carefully hidden by long grass.

By all accounts, Mary was a very pretty child with an abundance of curly, blonde hair. The children of the area were still on their midsummer break from school and they erected little stone houses around the place where Mary's body was found.

Mary was buried on the afternoon of 21 August at Heworth Cemetery with the service conducted by the Reverend Dr Steel. The whole district was deeply shocked by what had happened and there was a very large attendance at the funeral.

An initial inquest was carried out on 19 August at the Wesleyan school room to ascertain the circumstances of Mary's disappearance and the cause of death. Deputy Coroner A T Shepherd said he did not intend to go into the case fully until the police had time to complete their investigations. The police, after some initial enquires, arrested a young man in connection with the crime. He was Thomas Nicholson who was twenty-three and lived at Ann Street, Bill Quay. He worked as a cartman for a farmer in the area, Mr Robert Davidson.

A second inquest was held a few days later with more details coming to light. Dr J W Mackay from Pelaw had carried out an examination on the body. His findings were that the child had been hit sharply over the head, which may have caused unconsciousness. There were wounds on the head, arms and skin that had been caused by a blunt instrument either after the loss of a lot of blood or after death, he could not be sure. Marks around the nostrils and mouth were due to throttling with the right hand, not severe enough to strangle but perhaps to keep the child from shouting out. Mary had been lying on her back when a large instrument held in the right hand had been used on her lower body. In the doctor's opinion this was to allow easier penetration of a male organ. There were also other severe wounds to the lower part of her body. Dr Mackay's conclusion was that Mary had been seriously and violently sexually assaulted but had ceased struggling or was already dead when the worst wound was inflicted. She had died from choking on her own blood due to the throttling and probably the shock of the pain from the wounds inflicted to her lower body.

The county analyst, William F Stock, had examined the child's clothes and also the clothes belonging to Nicholson. Mary's clothes were saturated with water making the analyst's task extremely difficult. He had no trouble, however, in tracing bloodstains on her petticoats, chemise and drawers. He could find no trace of semen on any of the clothing. A pocket knife given to him by the police was also examined. There was blood on the blade but the analyst could not say how long it had been there. Mr Stock also found bloodstains on Nicholson's coat and trousers but none on the waistcoat. Nicholson's explanation was that he had had a nosebleed and his friend's wife, Mrs Dinning, had put a cold key down his back to stop the bleeding.

Witnesses gave evidence as to Nicholson's whereabouts on that Saturday. He and another man, James Dinning, had been drinking at the *Wardley Hotel* in the afternoon and had then gone to the *Mason's Arms* at Felling Shore. The two men had separated at Dinning's house a little before 7.30 on Saturday evening. Nicholson had then been seen, a little under the influence of drink, entering his own house and leaving about five minutes later to walk in the direction of the Hilly Fields. James Dinning went back out that evening. Mrs Dinning stated that Nicholson came to her house at about 9.30 on Saturday evening to ask if her husband was in. She said that she knew nothing about a nose bleed and did certainly not put a key down Nicholson's back. Mrs Dinning also added that Nicholson was wearing different clothes to the ones he had been wearing when he and Dinning had parted company earlier. Other witnesses had also seen Nicholson near to the Hilly Fields which was the route Mary would have taken to reach home. Thomas Nicholson was charged with murder and was sent to stand trial at the Durham Autumn Assizes.

At the trial the evidence was presented. Although it was all circumstantial, with no absolute proof that the blood on Nicholson's clothes belonged to the little girl, the jury took just thirty-five minutes to find him guilty of the wilful murder of Mary Ina Stewart. Justice Channell sentenced the prisoner

Durham Assize Court where Thomas Nicholson stood trial for murder. The author

to death. Nicholson never confessed to the crime but apparently accepted the judgment and his fate with no show of emotion.

On 16 December Thomas Nicholson, by then aged twenty-four, was hanged by William and John Billington at Durham. On the same day Samuel Walton was hanged for a triple murder at Middlestone Moor (See *Foul Deeds and Suspicious Deaths In & Around Durham*).

CHAPTER 31

More Executions at Morpeth and Newcastle
1305–1842

Many events have been recorded throughout the centuries, but some with very little detail. The following is a list of some of the executions carried out at Morpeth and Newcastle and some of the foul deeds that have taken place over the years other than those related in the previous chapters of this book.

1305: William Wallace, after having being executed at Smithfield, one of his quarters was displayed at Newcastle.

1306: John De Seyton hanged at Newcastle for taking part in the death of John Comyn.

The Castle Keep in 2003. Built by Henry II in 1168-78 on the site of the New Castle built in 1080 by Robert Curthose. Many felons were imprisoned and executed in this formidable building. The Castle is now a museum and tourist attraction. Author's collection

1322: One quarter of the body of Andrew de Hartela, Earl of Carlisle, executed for treason, was displayed on the Keep of the Castle.

1415: The head of Sir Thomas Grey, executed for treason, was placed on one of the gates of Newcastle.

1461, 1 May: James Butler, Earl of Wilts and Ormond, was beheaded at Newcastle.

1464: William Tallboys, Earl of Kent, was beheaded at Newcastle.

1547, 28 August: A group of soldiers, in the army of the Duke of Somerset, were hanged in Newcastle Market Place for 'quarrellyng and fightying.'

1565: Hugh Partridge was hanged for 'coyninge fals monnys in the Great Innes in Pilgrim Street'.

1593, 7 January: Edward Waterson a Roman Catholic priest, a native of London, was beheaded at Newcastle.

1593, 27 July: Joseph Lampton, a Roman Catholic priest, born at Malton in Yorkshire, was executed at Newcastle; he was of the ancient family of Lampton, South Biddick, in the County of Durham.

1594, Thomas Boast, a priest was hanged.

1599: Clement Roderforthe, gentleman, hanged in the Castle.

1603, 22 June: Brian Spore was hanged for stealing a velvet cloak.

1604, 17 April: In the register of All Saints, Newcastle. 'Buried Dame Whittingham, murthered by hir husband'. Sir Timothy Whittingham, son of Dean Whittingham is reputed to have slain three wives. Sir Timothy lived long after this fact extremely respected and he was appointed provost marshal to the levies in the County of Durham, being recommended by the bishop as an ancient knight and a severe justicer.

1604, 13 August: Six prisoners were buried at St Nicholas' Church.

1605, 12 May: Alexander Davison was 'hanged in the hye Castle' and buried at St John's Church.

1605, 14 November: Renold Charlton, Henry Dodds and Archie Dodds were hanged at the Castle and buried at St John's Church.

A 1914 sketch by Robert JS Bertram of All Saints Church.

1606, 25 January: John Hall, Archie Armstrong, Thomas Armstrong, Cuthbert Charlton, William Charlton and another whose name is not recorded were executed at the Castle and buried at St John's Church.

1611, 30 July: Bartram Potts and William Elwode buried at St John's Church.

1613, 23 April: Archie Read and John Robson buried at St John's Church.

A 1914 sketch by Robert JS Bertram of the church of St Nicholas from the Groat Market. Author's collection

1616, 1 August: Younghusbande, for the murder of Mr Swenna, gent, was executed at Newcastle.

1620, 13 August: Nicholas Forster for the murder of Mr Swenno was hanged.

1622, 17 August: John Driden, Yeoman.

1628, 18 August: Buried at All Saints Nick Nickson, taylor, executed.

1628, 19 August: Buried at St Nicholas three denisons, without name, hanged for murder.

1632, 13 August: Seventeen prisoners buried at St Nicholas, Church.

1636, 30 December: Rainald Murray executed for the murder of George Bower.

1639, 13 August: Executed, John Anderson, James Oswald Browne, George Ranson, Thos Debdel and Annas Hall.

1640, 16 May: Anthony Viccars, one of 'two sogers who had denied the King's pay'. The culprits were called upon to decide by ballot which of the two should die and Vicars, having drawn the lot, was set up against a wall in the 'Bigg Markett and shott by 6 lyght horsemen'.

1645, 3 August: Will Hall, Will Mor, Archibald Henderson and John Grame hanged at the Castle.

1649, 3 August: Stephen Milburn, John Hunter, Edward Hunter, Edward Hedley, Edward Sharper, Reinold Twadell, Edward Marleson, Robert Eilet, Joseph Robson, Edward Gram, John Foster, John Prudow, Edward Browne, Thos Reed, George Cock, John Robson, John Flecher, Alex Armstrong, John Linsley, Thomas Johnson and Humphrey Sotheran hanged, apparently border offenders.

1701, 25 September: John Fenwick JP was hanged for stabbing to death Fernando Forster MP. The two had quarreled at an Assize dinner being held at the *Black Bull* in Newgate Street.

St John's Church and churchyard in the eighteenth century. Author's collection

Old houses in Newgate Street in the nineteenth century. Author's collection

1715, 17 February: Henry Peltier, a soldier, was shot.

1733: Two men were hanged on the moor.

1739, 4 September: Michael Curry and John Wilson were executed at the Westgate, Newcastle. Curry had murdered Robert Shevill. He admitted his guilt. After he was hanged his body was taken to Hartley and hung in chains. Wilson had murdered Barbara Trumble whose husband, William, was a publican. He denied any knowledge of the event saying that it must have happened in a drunken affray at Trumble's public house. Wilson was interred in ground behind St John's Church.

1739, 14 September: William Smith was executed on the Town Moor, Newcastle for the murder of his wife. He made a confession to the Reverend Mr Wilkinson and then withdrew it when the rope was about to be placed around his neck. He asked that his clothes be given to his thirteen-year old son who had stood beside him when he was executed.

1742, 24 September: At Morpeth, John Todd for sheep stealing and William Simpson for felony.

1743, 8 August: William Brown, commonly called Sir William Brown, was at the head of a gang of thieves or moss-troopers had been convicted and sentenced to transportation

A view over the Town Moor to the chimney mills. Author's collection

from which he returned. He was tried at the Assizes at the Moot Hall in Newcastle and sentenced to death. Brown begged to be transported again but his request was denied. He used foul language to all in the court. Two companies of soldiers escorted him to Westgate for his execution for fear his cronies would try and rescue him.

1744, 11 August: James Maben, John Samuel and Thomas Lister were executed at the Westgate in Newcastle, the first two for coining and buried in the one grave, the last for horse stealing. Maben left an account of some of his misfortunes, which was later printed and sold for a penny a copy.

1746, 15 September: Alexander Anthony, aged twenty-three, a soldier, hanged on the Town Moor for entering the service of the King of France.

1751, 21 August: Richard Brown, a keelman, was executed on the Town Moor at Newcastle for the murder of his seventeen-year-old daughter by throwing her down the stairs. Brown alleged he was under the influence of drink at the time and had not meant to take her life.

1754, 7 August: Dorothy Catinby, of Love Lane on the quay at Newcastle, was executed on the Town Moor for the

The church of St Nicholas in 2003. The author

murder of her bastard child. She denied the crime to the end. Catinby was a widow and she was the mother of three lawful children. After her death her two sons drowned themselves and her daughter left her employment in service and moved away from Newcastle.

1758, 20 February: William Bland, a soldier who had been impressed into the service, deserted and was shot on the Town Moor.

1761, 5 October: Peter Patterson executed at Morpeth for high treason.

1764, 8 July: In the early hours of Sunday morning Robert Lindsey, a keelman, was on the wall in a lane in Sandgate near to George Stewart's house. Stewart was a pawnbroker. Stewart's wife, suspecting that Lindsey was going to rob their premises, told him to get off the wall and go away. When he refused she struck at him from her window with a pair of tongs. Lindsey became angry and broke some of the windowpanes. A quarrel ensued and Stewart took a loaded gun and fired it at Lindsey. The gun only flashed so Stewart's wife brought more powder and primed the weapon. Stewart then shot Lindsey killing him instantly. The couple was tried for murder and Stewart was executed on the Town Moor on 27 August 1764.

1764, 3 September: James Edgar, a cobbler, was executed at the Westgate for larceny and burglary in the house of Edward Bigg in West Jesmond near Newcastle. Edgar was clothed only in a shroud and was attended by four ministers. His accomplices were said to be Thomas Harrison, a hawker, his reputed wife, Isabella, and Andrew Simpson, Isabella's son, who was eight. The boy was put in the window first so he could unlock the door. The accomplices were acquitted.

1765, 29 July: Elizabeth Renwick, an elderly woman, was murdered in her son's house at Newbrough near Hexham. The rest of the family was out in the hay field at the time. The woman's blood was all over the house and the perpetrators had taken £58.

1765, 15 August: Joseph Hall, a soldier in the 6th Regiment, for firing a pistol in the face of William Cuthbertson, a Newcastle hairdresser, and burning his face.

1774, 20 August: George Davidson at Morpeth for rape.

1776, 21 August: Robert Knowles, a North Shields postman, was executed on the Town Moor for stealing a letter out of the Newcastle post office. The letter contained two £20 bills and was the property of Robert Rankin, a merchant. Knowles escaped from gaol by overpowering the turnkey. He was recaptured after a reward of twenty guineas (£23) was offered for information on his whereabouts.

On the same day Andrew MacKenzie, a soldier, was executed at Westgate for robbing a man named Temple on the North Shield road. A young butcher, William Robson, attended Knowles execution and then Mackenzie's. At the second execution he collapsed and died.

1783, 17 November: William Alexander was executed on the Town Moor for forging a bill of exchange. He was interred at St Andrew's churchyard.

1784, 26 August: James Chambers and William Collins, both sailors, were executed on the Town Moor for robbing Mr Jasper Anderson of Coxlodge.

1785, 16 August: William Graham for housebreaking and William Cockburn for horse stealing, at Morpeth.

1786, 30 August: Henry Jennings was executed on the Town Moor for horse stealing. During his execution a boy, Peter Donnison, was apprehended picking the pocket of a gentleman standing near to the gallows.

1787, 30 January: In St John's churchyard at Newcastle some workmen came upon a headless corpse covered in a bloodstained cloth. The body was determined to be of a girl of about fifteen who had been dead about twelve months. A reward was offered for information as to who the girl was and to her murder. Several people were questioned but no information was forthcoming. Neither the murderer nor the girl's head were ever found.

1788, 9 August: John and Robert Winter (father and son) were executed on Fair Moor (near Morpeth) for breaking into the house of William Charlton.

1789, 15 February: On Sunday John Elliott, a whitesmith, entered a public house in Newcastle and began verbally abusing several of the patrons. One of the men, Thomas Atkinson a tailor, made a retort back. Elliott threw a mug of beer into Atkinson's face and then ran out of the room. The patrons followed and a scuffle ensued. Elliott was found bruised and with a badly broken leg. Gangrene set in and Elliott died in agony on Wednesday. He left a wife and three children. At the Newcastle Assizes Atkinson was found guilty of manslaughter, fined 6s 8d (34p) and discharged.

1789, 26 August: Thomas Young, aged twenty-four, at Morpeth for highway robbery.

1789, 15 November: The body of thirty-year-old Ann Brown was

A 1914 sketch by Robert JS Bertram of St John's Church. Author's collection

found in Stepney Lane, Newcastle. She had been mangled in a manner too shocking for relation. Two men were arrested but after some weeks released without charge. Fletcher Reynoldson and Robert Gray were then arrested. They both confessed to being present when the murder was done but each blamed the other with the actual deed. At their trial at the Assizes in August 1790 no bill was found.

1790, 5 August: Thomas Watson, on a temporary gallows at Westgate, for the murder of a farmer, George Gibson

1790, 18 August: John Brown, at Morpeth, for horse stealing.

1793, 14 August: Walter Clarke, father of Jane and Eleanor Clarke (see chapter 4) and Margaret Dunn, at Morpeth for burglaries.

1800, 14 June: A mariner from Lynn named Wilkinson had to resort to begging from houses in Newcastle. He came to the house of Mr Moffatt, who looked after horses in Pilgrim Street

Mr Moffatt was not at home but Mrs Moffatt gave Wilkinson some bread, cheese and a small beer. She then presented her guest with a hatchet and asked if he would be kind enough to cut her fingers off as they gave her great pain. The astonished man at first refused but at Mrs Moffatt's insistence he lifted the hatchet and brought it down upon her hands. Two fingers of one hand and three of the other were severed. Mrs Moffatt was known to have occasional fits of insanity.

1801, 18 November: John Scott, at Morpeth, for sheep stealing.

1802, 23 August: John Carleton was executed at Durham. He and other accomplices had tried to forcibly enter a warehouse in Gateshead belonging to Thomas Greenwell, a grocer. Carleton had shot Greenwell with a pistol. The accused said that the pistol was not loaded so there had been no intention of murder. A week after the execution a bullet was found in the wall where the killing had taken place.

1802, 19 November: John Scott was executed at Morpeth for sheep stealing from Mr S Dodd.

1805, 16 August: Thomas Clare, a private in the 2nd Staffordshire Militia, at Westgate, for the murder of William

St John's Church in 2003. The author

Todd. This was the last execution to be carried out at Westgate.

1808, 1 September: Martin O'Bryan, at Morpeth, for robbing and cutting the throat of Barbara Weir on the Shields Road.

1809, 19 August: John Boyd, a man of twenty years, was executed at Morpeth for a forgery on the Durham Bank. He had respectable connections in Ireland but went to the gallows under an assumed name so as not to bring shame on his family.

1816, 7 September: James O'Neil was executed on the Town Moor at Newcastle for robbing Mr George Angus. The robbery took place in the preceding October as Angus was returning from the Cow Hill fair along the highway. O'Neil's body was taken by his friends to a public house to be waked and then interred at St Andrew's Church.

1817, 3 December: Charles Smith was executed on the Town Moor for the murder of Charles Stuart. His body was given to the surgeons for dissection.

1819, 14 April: Joseph Charlton, aged twenty-four, at Morpeth, for an unnatural crime.

1821, 10 September: John Wilkinson and William Surtees Hetherington, at Morpeth for robbing a farmer, William Nesbitt.

1822, 20 March: Mark Lawson and William Currie, at Morpeth for highway robbery.

1840, 26 June: William Blagburn, who was a sober man, had left his pregnant wife because of her excessive drinking. He went to visit his wife at Sandgate, Newcastle to ask how much she had received when she had pawned his clothes. She became aggressive and Blagburn struck her in the chest. His wife died shortly after. Blagburn first went up Pandon Bank and then to Heaton Wood, it was thought to commit suicide. The following morning he gave himself up. Blagburn was sentenced to ten months hard labour.

1840, 26 September: Martha Williams, an elderly woman, lived with her daughter and son-in-law, William Cowley, at Pandon Bank Newcastle. On Sunday morning a quarrel broke out between the couple. Cowley threw a pot of coffee at his wife and she threw one back at him. Cowley became enraged and picked up a poker. As he went to hit his wife, Martha intervened and received a violent blow to the head. The old woman died the following Sunday. At the Newcastle Spring Assizes in 1841 Cowley was found guilty of manslaughter and sentenced to ten years transportation.

1841, 11 August: As a man, named Bell, was passing along the Quayside at Newcastle at about 1 am he was accosted by two women. One of the women, Donnison, begged money from Bell. As they were talking Bell heard a scuffle further up the lane. On going to investigate he found a woman lying in a pool of blood. A man was standing beside her and he asked Donnison to give him a hand to take the woman to her lodgings. Bell went for a policeman and when they returned the man was gone. The woman was Jane Anderson and she had died because of a violent blow to the head. Donnison was accused, arrested and tried for murder but released through insufficient evidence.

1841, 14 September: Richard Robson and John Maclean were employed by Abbott and Garland of Gateshead. A fight broke out between the two men at Elswick Haughs near Newcastle. Maclean died as a result of the injuries he sustained. In spring of 1842 Robson was found guilty of manslaughter, but as murder was not the intention and he had already served six months in gaol, he was sentenced to a further one week's imprisonment.

1842, 22 February: On Tuesday afternoon James Robertson returned to work at Edward Lumsdon and Son, Strand Street, Monkwearmouth under the influence of alcohol. The foreman, James Liddle, remonstrated with him. Robertson picked up a sledge hammer and hit the foreman over the head with it. A second blow was aimed at the fallen man but fellow workmen managed to divert the blow. Liddle died a few hours later. He left a wife and eight children. Robinson originally came from Gateshead. He was twenty-seven and a widower. At his trial on Wednesday, 14 July 1842 he was found guilty of manslaughter and sentenced to transportation for life.

Sources

Reid's *Handbook to Newcastle-Upon-Tyne*, 1908

Historical Register of Remarkable Events, Volumes I–II, John Sykes, AD 800–1832

Historical Register of Remarkable Events, Volumes III–IV, T Fordyce, 1833–75

Borderer's Table Book, Volumes I-VI, M A Richardson, AD 800–1842

Local Records of Stockton and Neighbourhood, T Richmond, 1868

Haydn's *Dictionary of Dates*, 1873

South Durham Herald, 1866

South Durham and Cleveland Journal, 1901

The Evening Chronicle, 1901

Newcastle Weekly Chronicle, 1861, 1863, 1874, 1875, 1890, 1898, 1902

Newcastle Daily Chronicle, 1863, 1866, 1876, 1886, 1898

Newcastle Journal, 1859, 1869, 1870, 1872, 1875, 1894, 1897

Many of the illustrations in my collection are taken from plates within historical record books that I have within my collection.

174

Index

Places
Aberdeen, 45
Adelaide Hotel, 38
Alkali Inn, 98
Ann Street, 156
Askew Road, 148

Back Lane, 74
Barber's Hall, 21
Barley Moor, 42
Barrack Road, 35, 38, 132
Barracks, The, 45
Bay Hotel, 152–153
Bellgrave Hotel, 131
Bell Street, 36
Bentinck, 131
Benton Lane, 96
Benwell, 20
Berwick, 45, 72, 96
Bigg Market, 20
Bill Quay, 155–156
Black Bull Inn, 21–22, 97, 132
Blackett Street, 102–103, 149
Black Lion Inn, 34
Black Swan Inn, 134
Blandford Street, 76
Blenheim Street, 128–129
Blue Posts, 60
Blue Quarries, 121
Blyth Nook, 71
Blyth Square, 54
Botany Bay, 66
Broadway, 141
Buckingham Street, 109
Burn Bank, 69
Byker, 147
Byker Hill, 97

Caistron, 58
Cannon Street, 144–145
Carliol Square, 28, 79–80
Carrgate Inn, 139
Carr Hill, 121
Castle Keep, 44, 46–48
Castle Garth, 42, 61
Cat Dene Quarry, 155
Cellar's Entry, 67
Charlton's, 126
Chester le Street, 58
Church Gare, 18
Churchill Street, 129
Church Walk, 90
Clive Street, 34
Clogger's Entry, 78
Cockle Park, 94
Coldrife, 23
Corbridge, 45
Cowgate, 71
Cowpen Colliery, 54
Cox's Char, 68
Crescent Tavern, 142
Crooked Billet, 144
Cross Street, 141
Cullercoats, 151, 154

Darlington, 117
Dean Street, 64, 70–72
Dinnington, 136, 139
Dinnington Church, 139
Dog Kennel Field, 96
Drury Lane, 126
Dumfries, 144
Dunston, 14

Durham, 16–17, 41, 54, 57, 117, 123, 149–150, 158

East Adelaide Street, 80
East Terrace, 118, 144
Eldon Lane, 74
Elford, 23
Elsdon, 39–40
Elswick, 118, 144

Fair Moor, 45
Felling, 121, 157
Flesh Market, 22
Fourstones, 34
Friars' Goose Colliery, 54
Fulwell Lime Works, 50

Gallowgate, 30, 74
Gardner's House Farm, 136
Gateshead, 11, 14, 18, 37, 58, 86–87, 121, 125, 132, 147–148
General Moor, 133
Glasgow, 109
Glass House, The, 30
Gosforth, 146
Gosforth Terrace, 155
Grainger Street, 126
Grey's Monument, 102, 104–105, 107
Guildhall, 29, 61

Half Moon Inn, 134
Harbottle, 58
Harlow Hill, 40
Heathery Shank Farm, 133
Hebburn Quay, 29
Hedley Fell, 41
Hetton Colliery, 53
Heworth Cemetery, 156
Hexham, 33, 155
High Friar Street, 58
Highlander Inn, 69
High Street, 37
Hilly Fields, 155
Hindhaugh Street, 36, 132
Holy Saviour's Church, 142
Holystone, 58
Hopetown, 117
Horsley, 40
Horton Grange, 136
Huddleston Road, 151–152, 154
Hudson Street, 142
Hudspeth, 40

Ireland's, 109

Jarrow, 97
Jarrow Memorial Hospital, 97
Jesmond, 86
Joel Terrace, 155

Keelman's Hospital, 25–26
Kirtley Hall, 46

Laing's Hill, 40
Landshott, 40
Leicestershire, 57
London, 47
Long Benton, 96–97
Low Bridge, 71
Low Street, 34

Manor's Police Court, 106, 131
Marine Hotel, 135
Marlborough Street, 129
Mason's Arms, 157
Matfen, 100
Middlesbrough, 68
Middlestone Moor, 158
Milling Street, 147–149
Mill House Lane, 131
Mitford, 41
Mitford Street, 82–83
Moot Hall, 17, 42–43, 61–62, 151–152
Morpeth, 34, 41–42, 45, 55, 57, 66, 94–95, 97, 140
Mosely Street, 71

Nag's Head, 114
Netherwitton, 45
Newbrough, 33
Newbrough Lodge, 33
Newcastle, 9–13, 25, 27, 29, 35, 43, 45, 50, 52–53, 55, 57–59, 67–68, 70, 75–76, 82–84, 86, 96, 109, 114, 117–118, 125, 128, 130, 136–138, 140, 143–144, 147, 151, 154
Newcastle Arms, 79
Newcastle Gaol, 13, 71, 112, 145, 154
Newcastle Infirmary, 32, 36, 50, 133, 138
Newcastle Police Court, 91–92
Newcastle Railway Station, 128
Newcastle Savings Bank, 59–62
Newgate Gaol, 13, 28, 89
Newgate Street, 27, 38, 41
Newham, 23, 46
New Quay, 35
North Mill Lane, 131
North Shields, 34, 58, 151
Northumberland, 11, 23, 30, 45, 58, 62, 101, 137, 140, 151
Northumberland Street, 102
Nun Street, 126

Ocean Road, 135
Ouseburn, 58
Ouseburn Pottery, 50
Ovingham, 41

Pandon, 69
Pele House, 39–40
Pelaw, 155
Percy Street, 58, 74
Pilgrim Street, 59–60, 71, 90–91
Pine Street, 84
Pink Lane, 71
Pipwellgate, 30, 86
Ponteland, 46, 138
Portland Arms, 94
Portland Street, 131
Prince's Street, 71
Prudhoe Street, 104

Quayside, 68

Raw, The, 39
Redheugh Bridge, 147
Robertsons, 77
Rothbury, 58
Ryton, 41

Index175

Sandgate, 63, 67
Scotland, 9, 12, 14, 17
Scotswood, 125
Scotswood Road, 144
Seaton Burn, 56
Sedgefield Lunatic Asylum, 123
Side, 63–64, 77–79
Silver Street, 115
Six Mile Bridge, 56–57
Shieldfield, 130
South Shields, 80–81
Spicer's Lane, 68
Split Crow Lane, 122
St Andrew's Church, 12, 27, 29, 32–33, 70
Stepney Lane, 130
Steng Cross, 45
St Mary's Church, 17
St Nicholas' Church, 17
Stowell Street, 112
Strensall, 141
Sunderland, 50

Town Moor, 11, 13, 20, 24–25, 51–52, 146
Tyne, River, 125
Tyne Bridge, 14
Tyne Bridge, 14–17
Tynedale, 42
Tyne Main Colliery, 54
Tynemouth, 119, 141–142
Tyneside Terrace,

Wapping, 134
Wardley Hotel, 157
Waterloo, 100
Waterloo Inn, 43
Waterloo Street, 126
West Bromwich, 141
Westgate, 23–24, 43, 76, 110, 112, 119, 129
Westminster Street, 37
West Walls, 110–111
Williamson's Road, 122
Willington George Pit, 96
Windsor Hotel, 36–37
Westmoreland Road, 118
Whitlees, 40
Whitley Bay, 141
Whiskerfield, 40, 45
Winlaton,116
Woolpack Inn, 129

York, 58, 141

People
Addison, Edward Adams, 36
Alderman, Mr, 59
Alderson, Baron, 61
Allan, Ellen, 100
Allan, Isabella, 100
Allan, Jane, 100
Allan, Michael, 100
Anderson, Elsabeth, 10
Anderson, Elizabeth, 82–84
Anderson, John William, 82–84
Anderson, PC George, 105
Angus, Dr, 131
Armstrong, John, 10
Armstrong, Dinah, 14–19
Armstrong, George, 10
Armstorng, Jane, 16
Armstrong, Simend, 10
Armstrong, Tamar, 16
Arnott, Thomas, 139
Arrowsmith, Samuel, 34
Askern, Thomas, 112
Atkins, Fredrick, 128–129

Atkinson, Charles, 149
Aynsley, Michael, 46–47, 49
Ayrey, Sergeant Thomas, 81

Baird, Colonel, 45
Baker, William, 71
Barlow, Joseph, 146
Bathurst, Justice, 17
Batson, Alderman, 61
Baumgarter, Dr, 91
Beale, Mr, 125
Bennett, Margaret, 137
Berry, James, 86
Bewicke, Dorothy, 100
Billington, James, 154
Billington, John, 158
Billington, Thomas, 150, 154
Billington, William, 90, 150, 158
Blackett, Edward, 100
Blackwell, Mr, 112
Bleckinsopp, William, 97
Bramwell, Baron, 140
Bramwell, Dr, 120
Brown, Henry, 31–32
Brown, Isabell, 9
Brown, John, 31
Brown, Margrit, 9
Brown, PC, 35
Brown, William, 10
Bolam, Archibald, 58–66
Boumer, Matthew, 10
Bowman, George, 37
Boyd, Captain, 133
Boyle, Mrs, 149
Bramwell, John, 98
Brindle, Samuel, 72–73
Brown, Isabell, 10
Brown, John, 40
Brown, Margrit, 10
Brown, Thomas, 132–133
Bryson, Mrs, 96
Buckam, 111
Buddle, William, 55–57
Burns, Joseph, 121

Carlisle, Elizabeth, 92
Carlisle, Martha, 92
Casely, PC, 113–115
Carr, Cuthbert Rodham, 121–124
Carr, Dr, 76
Cattermole, William, 74–75
Chambers, Fenwick, 74
Channell, Justice, 157
Charles, Justice, 143
Charlton, James, 46–47, 49
Charlton, Joseph, 138
Charlton, Richard, 136–138
Charlton, Sarah, 136–138
Clark, Edward, 146
Clark, George, 102–108
Clarke, Eleanor, 42–43, 45
Clarke, Jane, 41–43, 45
Clarke, William, 45
Clarkson, Dr, 117
Claydon, Mrs, 145
Coleridge, Justice,
Conner, John, 97–98
Conner, Michael, 97–99
Connolly, Mrs, 86
Conroy, James, 100
Coombes, Mrs, 117
Cope, Albert Edward, 119–120
Cope, John, 119
Cope, Mrs, 119–120
Copperthwaite, Mary, 134–135
Cosser, John, 36–37
Cowens, Robert, 131
Creighton, Mr, 95

Cross, Dr, 85
Crowther, Mrs, 126
Crozier, Margaret, 39–40, 43

Dalrymple, John, 103–105
Dalrymple, Mrs, 38
Danskin, Kit, 83
Davidson, PC, 140
Davidson, Robert, 156
Dawson, Ivy, 147–149
Dees, Elizabeth, 77
Denham, Justice, 84
Dinning, James, 157
Dinning, Mrs, 157
Dobson, Elsabeth, 10
Docherty, John, 109–110
Docherty, Margaret, 109–112
Dodds, George, 83
Dodds, Sarah, 83
Dodds, William,
Donahoe, Christopher, 80–82
Donkin, John, 74
Dronweth, Jo, 10
Drummond, Barbara, 39
Dunn, Margaret, 45
Dykes, 31
Dykes, John, 80
Dykes, Margaret, 80–81

Ellis, John, 154
Ellison, Mary, 69
Ellot, 10
Emery, Samuel, 141–143
Errington, John, 53–54
Errington, Thomas, 30–32
Erskine, Dr William, 14
Eustice, Jane, 113
Eustice, Michael, 113–115
Eustice, Mr, 113–114
Eustice, Thomas, 113, 115

Fagan, Daniel, 90–93
Fagan, Elizabeth, 90, 93
Fagan, Mary, 118–119
Fenning, John Henry, 70–73
Ferguson, Joseph, 151–153
Ferguson, Mrs, 151, 153
Forbes, Bridget, 77
Forbes, Elizabeth, 77
Forbes, Patrick, 77–80
Forbes, Thomas, 77
Forster, Catherine, 122
Fothergill, JR Dr, 117
Frater, Mark, 102–107
Froggat, Dr, 35

Gardner, William, 43
Gibson, George, 23, 142
Gillespie, 111
Gouin, George, 58
Graham, John, 97
Grainger, Mr, 116
Grant, Mr, 31
Grantham, Justice, 151
Green, Rev Robert, 28
Grey, PC Alex, 90
Grey, Francis, 25
Guise, General, 20

Hackney, Robert, 36–38
Hall, Elizabeth, 116–117
Hall, Mr, 117
Hall, Mrs, 117
Hall, William, 40
Hand, Annie, 90–93
Hayes, James, 34–35
Heath, Dr, 138
Hedley, Dr, 94–95